mantras

THE SACRED CHANTS

Swami Veda Bharati

mantras

The Sacred Chants

wisdom tree

First published 2008
Reprinted 2011, 2013

ISBN 978-81-8328-094-5

Published by
Wisdom Tree
4779/23 Ansari Road
Darya Ganj, New Delhi-110002
Ph.: 23247966/67/68
wisdomtreebooks@gmail.com

Printed in India

contents

Preface vii
Introduction ix
1. Mantra: What and Why 1
2. Difference Between Sutra and Mantra 24
3. Mantra After Initiation 41
4. Special Mantras 76
5. Refining Your Mantra 95
Appendix 106
Some Mantras to Chant 110

preface

"May we recite the mantra for fire," prayed the *rishi* in the *Rg-Veda.* The fire is to be invoked and kindled within the *kunda*, the fire-vessel within us.

The fire invoked through the mantra burns all our dross and macula, leaving us as burnished gold.

Only as golden beings can we enter the *hiranya-garbha,* the golden womb of the cosmic field of intelligence, the universal ocean of wisdom, that is the first and the last guru.

Only as golden beings can we enter the space spoken of in the *Atharva-Veda* — within the transcendent gold treasury dwells the dustless, immaculate, incalculable, indivisible Brahman, that is the bright and clear light of lights that the self-knowers know.

The self-knowers then have free and full access to that which Patanjali has named as *tarakam jnanam*, the knowledge that helps us cross over from this shore to the 'that' which is beyond our day-to-day 'this'. Such knowledge is instantaneous, covers an entire field, is supra-logical and non-sequential. In that intuitive knowledge, the *mantric* phrases are not composed of words, nor are the words composed of syllables, nor are the syllables made up of phonemes. The entire knowledge flashes in on instant, *kshana*. A *kshana* is defined in the commentaries on the *Yoga Sutras* as the time it takes the minutest atomic particle to traverse the space of its own length and breadth, which simply is a point in space. Such knowledge, appearing as a ripple of wisdom, in the *rishi's buddhi* in a single *kshana* is called a mantra.

May you not be content with reciting the *mantras* verbally. A *yogi's* mantra recitation allows for no movement of the tongue or of the larynx; it must simply be a wave in the mind, a remembrance, *smaranam*. That wave too will subside and the entire being will get immersed in a lake of ecstatic silence.

I wish the reader the discovery of the infinite world of silence through the mantra.

In service of Gurudeva,

Swami Veda Bharati

Swami Rama's Ashram

Rishikesh

introduction

Raja yoga, the royal path, is the complete yoga that is taught in the *Yoga Sutra* of Patanjali, to which even the greatest authors on *hatha yoga*, such as Svatamarama, pay homage. Interpreted, expanded in practice and handed down in experiential and initiatory guidance by the Himalayan masters, it is referred to as the Himalayan tradition. However, without a live transmission, Patanjali cannot be understood. The first transmission to students, therefore, is of a mantra, a sonar unit, to concentrate upon.

one

MANTRA: WHAT AND WHY

The Word 'Mantra'

The word 'mantra' is related to the English words 'man', 'mind' and 'mental', which are derived from the Latin word *mens* (mind) and which in turn arises from the Greek word *menos* (mind). *Menos*, *mens*, mental, mind, man and mantra — all are derived from the Sanskrit verb root *man*, meaning 'to meditate'. Man is the living entity who can meditate as he has the mind with which to meditate. He focuses on a word, a mantra, for meditation. In India and in other parts of Asia, life without a mantra is like food without salt. One finds something missing in life. A human being is incomplete without a mantra.

What is a Mantra

A mantra is a word or a series of words; or it can be a

thought or a prayer, but not in the sense in which the word 'prayer' is used ordinarily. It is more like linking our lower consciousness with the higher consciousness, which we call Divine Consciousness, or the divine life-force. A mantra is a sound-unit, a thought-unit. It is a sound or a series of sounds given to a yoga student or disciple to remember constantly for a specific spiritual purpose. In the web of our consciousness, the energy of consciousness takes two forms — sound and light. At a certain stage, the sound and light energy entwine or unify. At the existing stage of our growth, they are experienced differently from each other. So we begin our initiation with the sound of a mantra. The initiation into light comes a little later.

Initially there are two aspects to a mantra that need to be understood — one aspect is that it is a syllabic combination forming a sound that has a particular effect on the mind, especially if it is repeated mentally; and the second aspect is its meaning.

Effect of a Repeated Sound

The theory of mantra is based on the principle that the sounds, letters and syllables of the alphabets carry within them the focus of certain psychic or mental vibrations. Each syllable has within it a particular ray of consciousness. When we think of a particular letter of the alphabet or a combination of these letters, each produces certain thoughts and vibrations. There is a certain texture or flavour to the sound. The thought of a word is the vibration of the mind, but not all vibrations are alike. Different syllables carry the focus for the force of different vibrations. This is seen in a crude way in the sound produced by certain words. For example, let's suppose that I am in a foreign country where nobody speaks English. I am in a somewhat whimsical mood, and I walk out of my hotel room. I walk down the street, when I notice a person coming my way. He does not know English, yet I approach him and say harshly, "Thud!"

Okay, 'thud!' He does not know what it means, but the sound has some impact on his mind. The next day I feel bad at having scared the poor fellow and want to make up for it. So I walk out on the street and when I see a person approaching — this person too does not know English — I say softly, "Lull!" What is the difference between the two sounds? The sounds 'thud' and 'lull' are qualitatively different. Poets and skilled writers are well aware of this difference and use the words to greater effect in their compositions. This proves that a sound has an impact in itself, irrespective of its translation. It creates an impression on the mind. Similarly each mantra has its own distinct sound vibration.

Mantra as an Energy Force

We can proceed a little further. The entire universe is run

by conscious forces which can be either angels, or deities, or incarnations, or manifestations of God and so on and so forth. The mantras are representative of specific forms of consciousness. So we think of the mantras as sonar forms of the forces of Divinity. There are some traditions in Christanity, Sufism and in the Jewish Kabbalistic tradition where the name of God is considered God Himself.

To be more specific, each individual mind has its own composition. In the mind are stored imprints of many lifetimes. We call these imprints *samskaras.* No matter what action we perform, what desires we feel, what impulses arise in us, they are all activated by these imprints. These imprints, from the past, constitute our personality. If we want to refine ourselves, we need to learn to change the pattern of these imprints. If hot water is added to a glass half-filled with cold water, the character of the water changes. If I have imprints that lead to bitter thoughts and I pour in one central thought of a mind-sweetening sound over and over again every day for many hours a day, say for 10, 15 or 20 years, the mind receives its imprint and is bound to change. In a similar manner, the mantra changes our nature, making it more refined, gentler and quieter. If the totality of a person's imprints leads him to disturbed thoughts, he is given a quietening mantra. If the imprints are too passive, he is awarded an activating mantra. And as the mantra is remembered over and over again, the imprint of the same mantra brings about certain desirable changes in one's personality.

Being a name and the sonar body of Divinity, the mantra so imprints itself upon the mind's deeper layers that the 'human' gives way to the Divine. Meditation with mantra is akin to a wordless prayer and is the subtlest sentiment in the practice of devotion. It is the ultimate in saying 'not mine', 'all thine', 'only thine', so that the entire personality may thereby become the abode of God, an instrument of the deity, a form through which Divinity alone may henceforth act, slowly but in due time. The practice for this begins when one ceases to 'recite' the mantra but only lets it arise from within.

Mantras Specific to Personalities and Purposes

There might be some people who may object and say, "Hey, I like myself as I am. I do not want to change my personality, and I don't want anyone to interfere with it." Even if you do not receive a mantra, the simple form of meditation, by withholding the breath and saying "*so-ham*", will bring about the required change in you. These are however not quite as effective as a personal mantra is. When a personal mantra, called a *diksha* (initiation) or a 'guru mantra', is given, it is like taking a drop from the universal mind of tradition and planting that drop, that seed, into the initiate's mind. It is called initiation because no matter how small it is, some form of energy is transmitted from the disciple to the recipient. In the *Brhadaranyaka Upanishad*, dated *circa* 14th century BC, we can read about a list of teachers of a particular lineage, giving details of each teacher having taught whom. Thus a list of 68 generations of teachers is given, with the first one being *Svyambhu Brahman*, the self-existent Supreme Being. "Pay homage to that self-existent Supreme Being," says the *Upanishad*. So mantras include sounds, thoughts, words — given as a revelation within the consciousness of the ancient *rihis* (sages) — in the highest state of *samadhi*, the ultimate meditation. The mantras are awakened within the soul as a revelation before they are passed down the line from the guru to the disciple, the initiate.

There are different mantras for different people. How does this work? Here we shall talk a little about the history of the yoga tradition. Sometimes people ask, "What is transcendental meditation (TM)? Where does TM fit into the yoga tradition?"

The word 'transcendental' is a modern expression. It is certainly not a Sanskrit word; it is a translation of something else.

Some people wonder, "How about Zen meditation? How does it compare with yoga meditation?"

Around 3000 BC, India was a country of pioneers, similar to what America was in the 1800s. People, migrating from many directions, felled trees in the wild forests, that covered the earth's surface, and settled down to establish cities and religions. But some, who were deeply philosophical, withdrew from all this to set up hermitages deep in forests and caves in the mountains. They took to the path of self-conquest, self-exploration. When men grew tired of the life in villages and cities and desired peace of mind, they decided to visit these hermit-teachers, the great masters, and would sit at their feet in the hope of receiving some peace of mind, a sense of direction and wisdom, before returning to their towns and villages to resume their normal worldly life. Some of these hermitages became great universities. For example, Alexander of Macedonia, who invaded India in the 4th century BC, came very close to the area near the university of Takshashila, which had over 20,000 students in residence at that time. Here learning was not divorced from spirituality. It invariably involved building the student's character. During student life (the *brahmacharya* stage), pupils were taught to conduct themselves in a manner that would render them useful to society and enable them to evolve spiritually.

The great masters of the Himalayas, who were founders of the yoga system and through whose intuitive knowledge and wisdom the teaching was and is still being spread, were experimental. We already know that the nature of our thoughts creates our personality. Usually we neither hold on to any 'single thought' nor do we think consistently. Our thoughts tend to run haphazardly. The practice of mantra involves the practice of focusing on a thought and dwelling on it consistently till it leaves a certain impact on the mind.

The great masters of the yoga tradition might say, "Son, you do not have enough fire in you. We'll give you a fire-mantra. Sit by a flame, a candle flame, and stare at it while holding your breath. Try to remember, or listen to, this particular fire-mantra. In six months' time, some changes will occur in your personality and these will be very positive." Another student might be told, "All you lack is the coolness and flow of water; so we'll give you the water-mantra to recite while you sit and meditate by the flowing waters." Over a period of time, that visual impress as well as that one thought which is remembered consistently with concentration, may bring very subtle changes in the student's personality.

Gradual Change in Personality

Changes in the human personality do not take place overnight. Before going to bed, take a look in the mirror to observe your face. On waking up the next morning, observe keenly if your face has changed overnight. It has not. It is the same face. Look at it again the following evening. You will find that, from morning to evening, it is the same face. The next morning, next evening, it is the same face. Five years or 10 years hence, compare yourself to your photograph of today. Observe the difference. Did you go to bed and wake up with a changed face? The changes in human personality are very subtle and imperceptible. People, who begin to practice meditation after receiving the mantra, soon become impatient because the mind changes very slowly. A person once called me over the phone and said, "I got my mantra three months ago. When do I get enlightenment?"

The process of progressing spiritually and undertaking a specific practice regularly is called *sadhana*. Generally this is a slow, gentle and gradual process. It cannot be rushed into because there is so much to assimilate. But human beings are impatient and want to get immediate results. But remember, there are no shortcuts to enlightenment.

Different Ways of Using the Mantra

There are many different pathways to the core of your consciousness. This is what meditation is all about. There are many different pathways to the real self, and there are different methods and techniques of meditation prescribed for different personalities. People may concentrate on a candle flame. Some may use particular breathing exercises; others may use a different breathing exercise. Some may listen to the sound of the mantra; some may concentrate on the mantra while music plays in the background; still others may be taught to concentrate on a given centre of consciousness while practicing the mantra.

Nowadays most people are taught to begin with simple mantras before proceeding to complex ones. Once in a while, for a certain period of time, a mantra may be practiced through internal concentration, or by making fire offerings which render it 10 times more intense. This practice casts an imprint of one particular thought on the mind. Through that imprint, a door opens somewhere and no matter where the seeker happens to be, his next step will take him closer.

Raja Yoga and Its Divergent Paths

The great masters, the founders of the Himalayan tradition of yoga, were aware of the different pathways leading to self-conquest, to self-exploration, to the core of our highest consciousness. However, not every disciple is capable of mastering all the different areas of meditation. Some persons may decide to practice only physical yoga for a long time; others may choose to concentrate on a particular sound; while still others may succeed in concentrating on light. They acquire mastery of specific systems within the larger system and establish their own academies and *ashrams*. Thus today there are different branches of yoga: *hatha yoga, nada yoga, laya yoga,* and so on and so forth. Students join certain *ashrams* and settle down to try out a particular path for a while. Now what happens is that some students begin to tell themselves, 'This is the best path.'

Why do they do this? Because it is good for them. It helps them. "I derive great benefit from it," they say.

But another person says, "Oh, these people! I have been there; I tried meditation but nothing happened to me."

Disciples of great masters attained mastery of specific systems, though very, very few were found capable of mastering the entire *raja yoga*, the royal path, the main path, which incorporated all the systems into a larger scheme. In *raja yoga* there is a greater diversity of methods, though all fall under the umbrella of the original system. All these systems fit within a scheme where there are many systems, methods and mantras suitable for different individuals. Thus in our tradition, we start with *raja yoga*, the royal path of yoga.

Initiation

What is initiation? It is said that the practices of yoga yoke all levels of our being into a unity. Similarly, initiation affects all the levels of our lives — physical, mental and spiritual. Let's see what initiation means on each of these levels.

Initiation on the Physical Level

On the physical level, initiation is a ritual marking a turning point in our life. With initiation, an individual becomes a student of a particular guru of yoga and places himself or herself under the direct tutelage of this spiritual master and other teachers practicing the same style of yoga. To some extent, being initiated is like becoming part of a family with the brothers and sisters as co-initiates and family elders as teachers.

As with all rituals, a prescribed pattern of action is performed by the initiator (teacher) and by the initiate (student). In the Himalayan tradition, the student may purify himself or herself during the day prior to the initiation by bathing, eating pure vegetarian food and cultivating serenity of mind. To the initiation ritual, the student brings *dakshina* (a monetary donation of a specific amount for the guru), and wears clean and comfortable clothing.

At the site of the initiation, the student sits quietly for a while before being led to the initiator/teacher who is engrossed in deep meditation. The teacher may guide the student into the meditation posture and relaxation. The teacher whispers a mantra into the student's right ear, and then the teacher and student may sit together and meditate for a while. The initiation ritual ends with a blessing to the student.

Initiation is a ritual of giving. The teacher gives a blessing, a word (mantra), and a commitment to help the student grow spiritually. The student in return learns the truth with an open mind. The student gets the opportunity to grow spiritually.

Initiation on the Energetic Level

On the energetic level, initiation has two aspects. It provides us with a glimpse of our goal and helps us to start its practice.

Normally it is seen that in the presence of a person who is experiencing strong emotions, the same emotions are aroused in us. For example, we might feel fear in the presence of one who is terrified and angry near the one who is enraged. This being so, imagine the effect of being near the one who is completely at peace! Sitting in the presence of such a person can soothe our nerves for a while, and give us a taste of another way of being. Then we can strive to attain a similar serenity on our own.

Beyond informing us of our goal, initiation gives us a push in the direction of our goal. Initiation is said to be an infusion of energy from the spiritual source. Thus, in religious art all over the world, initiation is depicted as rays of light falling upon the initiate, often from above. In this sense, initiation is a spiritual jump-start given to make our spiritual engine run. A teacher, who has attained a deeper level of meditation, transfers a bit of this state to the initiate and starts the practice. It is difficult to say more about this aspect of initiation because it is something that each person must experience and explore for herself or himself.

Initiation on the Level of Mind

In addition to affecting us on the physical and energetic levels, initiation affects our mind through the mantra. The mantra given at initiation can lead us towards inner peace. Here's how. Our minds are usually filled with random thoughts — some painful, some pleasant. If we focus on painful thoughts, we feel pain. If we shift our focus to pleasant thoughts, we feel pleased. Thus, by selectively attending to painful or pleasant thoughts, we cause ourselves to feel pain or pleasure.

Yoga takes this logic and extends it a step further. By concentrating on the peaceful mantra thought, we calm our minds and hearts to attain a state of serenity that is beyond pain or pleasure. Mantras are said to be pure sounds that evoke special qualities in our minds. Different mantras, like different musical sounds, affect us differently. The mantra given at initiation is selected to provide that something which the initiate needs.

When that mantra is repeated over and over by the initiate during meditation and throughout the day, the mind gets affected. The impact of rock'n roll music will be very different from that of listening to soft music. So too is the case with the mantra. The mantra is like a key; a key to the centre of our being. We turn that key by constant repetition of the mantra.

There is a second mental effect of initiation. To travel on the spiritual path, it is important to sharpen our ability to perform our actions skilfully and not create obstacles for ourselves. Sharpening our ability means refining that part of our mind which makes discriminations and is called *buddhi* in Sanskrit. Meditation upon our initiation mantra refines *buddhi* by enhancing our ability to witness undisturbed all that what happens around us. Over time, we enhance our ability to observe our usual patterns of thinking and distinguish our projections from reality. Thus, initiation affects our mind in a very beneficial manner.

Initiation on the Spiritual Level

Finally, initiation affects us on the spiritual level too, opening us to the ultimate source of wisdom, called *hiranyagarbha* (golden womb) in Sanskrit. *Hiranyagarbha* is the non-personal inner teacher, or guru, from which all embodied teachers draw their light. Initiation connects us with that guru.

Initiation: Expectation and Reality

Sometimes what seekers expect from initiation can

be unreasonable. It must be remembered that mantra initiation is the *first* initiation on the yogic path, not the last. Some newcomers to yoga expect to become enlightened right away, but this is not how things work. True, for some, self-realisation is instantaneous, but most of us may need to practice meditation for a long time to attain self-realisation. Even Yogi Muktananda, who was already an accomplished practitioner of yoga before receiving initiation from his guru, meditated for more than 10 years before attaining what he considered to be self-realisation.

Besides, what is the hurry? There is so much to learn and so many ways to grow that why should we demand to do it all at once? One might compare initiation to acquiring the ability to read and really enjoy it, and being given the opportunity to read all the books in an immense library. Of course, you can look forward to completing your task, but, you can also read at a particular speed, savouring each book.

Another point is that initiation alone won't result in enlightenment. Rather, one has to work towards self-realisation by indulging in spiritual practices and working towards purifying oneself. One needs to meditate to understand emotions, shun anger and overcome fear. This path is like one of those charities where every donation given is doubled or tripled by the sponsor of the charity — for it has been said that whatever spiritual work you do is reciprocated several times over by the source. But you have to do your part for something to happen. As Baba Hari Dass, a well known *yogi* in California, has written in his *Fire Without Fuel* (p. 79):"One who depends on fate or destiny and doesn't make any effort but remains sitting is like one who sits by the seashore waiting for a pearl to wash up."

One more thing — receiving initiation doesn't mean life will suddenly become easy and that all problems will be over. Remember, initiation aids in spiritual growth, and spiritual growth occurs by surpassing our limitations. Thus, as initiates, we often find ourselves involved in activities we avoided in the past. It is a common experience to discover the previously unrecognised inner strength, which sustains us in such situations. In addition, we have the comfort and companionship of other initiates and seekers of truth, and also the inspiration of teachers and sages. Strength is attained by confronting fear and developing the ability to serve and love, and not merely by indulging in wishful thinking.

In addition to the key to spiritual development, initiation also provides other benefits. Teachers take on the responsibility of guiding the initiate towards self-realisation. The ability to discuss one's practice with experienced teachers is an invaluable aid on the spiritual path, because very often a sage's advice is most helpful.

Also, if necessary, a person may be given certain practices to aid in spiritual work.

How are Mantras Chosen in Initiation?

A mantra is a syllable or a series of syllables appropriate for an individual person. Here a person might ask his initiator, "You hardly know my name. How can you choose a mantra for me?"

There are two different processes for acquring knowledge: a rational process and an intuitive process.

First of all, you must know who you are. Many people identify themselves with their names and believe they are their names. On the contrary, they are not what their name is. Where did their name come from? Let us presume that you take birth in a very advanced civilisation 3,000 years from now and where the people have only numbers, or where everybody keeps their name a secret. In such a scenario, all kinds of possibilities can arise. When you were born, you did not come out of your mother's womb and announced, "I am Mary." Maybe when you were one-and-a-half or two-years old, something in you said, 'They say the word Mary and they look at me'; or they say, 'Mary, come here. Mary, do this. Mary do that, hence my name must be Mary'. It is a conditioned reflex. Your name is not you.

There are certain personality types and understanding

this in itself constitutes a science. Each person has some strengths and some weaknesses. Those who understand the science of yoga are trained to look at the personality type because the mantra has to match the personality. The initiator is one who is trained in the science of mantra as also in the different aspects of human personality.

The process of initiation, however, goes far beyond this. The mantra is intuitively received by the initiator. The person who initiates is the one who has a very pure, unclouded, unblocked mind and, when meditating, he can receive and impart the mantra which will match the personality of the initiate. Now we are reluctantly entering an area which many people will not accept. Some may call it a mystery. You are free to accept or reject it, believe in it or not. Many people cannot accept that such an act of grace is possible and so they do not ask for a personal mantra. They take what they have learned about meditation as a unit. There are other helpful courses they can take, and may continue their practice of yoga on the basis of whatever they have learned. However, in our tradition, advanced practices of meditation are never given without first imparting the personal mantra.

The teacher, the initiator, will seldom say, "I want to give you a mantra." It is something that should arise from within you. If you feel the urge, you ask. Then a time is set and a very simple form of initiation takes place. But the urge has to come from within the would-be initiate's own consciousness. It has to be his own interior impulse. But, again, even if the impulse does not surge up within you, then at least set yourself a regular meditation time. Even setting up a fixed time for meditation will keep you in touch with the source of grace.

The Process of Initiation

The ceremony of initiation in the Himalayan tradition involves certain traditionally established procedures. Because it is a turning point in a student's life, the student is asked to purify himself /herself for at least a day prior to initiation. This is done by restricting oneself to a *sattvic* (pure) diet of vegetarian food and avoiding emotionally disturbing activities while cultivating serenity of the mind. The student then receives her/his mantra after bathing and dressing.

At the time of initiation itself, the student is asked to bring a gift of fruit and flowers along with the *dakshina.* These gifts are symbolic of the five senses — *rupa* (sight), *rasa* (taste), *gandha* (smell), *sparsha* (touch), *shabda* (sound), and indicate a student's sincere intention not to renounce sensual enjoyment, but to subordinate it to the greater benefits of spiritual upliftment.

The student is asked to sit quietly and meditate for some time. Then she/he is led to a room where the initiator is engaged in meditation. The student and teacher meditate together briefly before the mantra is conferred. Generally the mantra is whispered into the student's right ear, after which meditation is continued for a few more minutes. The ceremony ends with a blessing from the initator to the student. This is a process of giving and sharing at the highest level. The student gives his/her trust and willingness to seek the truth and embark on the journey of self-discovery (*sadhana*). The teacher, through the grace of gurus, gives the mantra and commitment to help the student to grow spiritually.

Mantra as a Stable Force in One's Life

The aim of the mantra is to have a special word within oneself. Some schools advise the use of mantra for only 20 minutes a day as taught in the *raja yoga*. Swami Rama advises you to make your mantra your personal friend. He asks you to keep the mantra in your mind at all times: whether standing at a bus stop, or waiting for an appointment, or driving a car, or when in need of focusing. Your mantra is yours; it is with you. It could be a word or phrase that should remain with you all the time. Normally all kinds of random thoughts and impressions clutter the mind as these are gathered from outside. A thought or impression from outside may excite you, aggravate you, disturb you, or frighten you. But the mantra is something that is yours; it's something from within. So while the whole world bombards you with disturbing impressions, the mantra within you should remain your permanent focus. This involves time to practice and master it so that it becomes your focus. It becomes a quiet friend to whom you can take recourse to deal with excitement and agitation. When you remember the mantra often enough, it becomes a part of your subconscious mind. The mantra can be your door to meditation because it is the focus, the focal point. The practice of mantra becomes meditation.

As you learn to use your mantra, and continue to use it, the method may be changed to take you further "up as until today you have done it *this* way. Now, you should move on to *that*." Sometimes nothing changes for years. But do not compare yourself with others. Nor should you feel that if someone else gets a different method, then you, too, should get a different method. The one method you have been given may be effective enough for you. It all depends on the individual and also upon the kind of relationship that she/he wants to maintain with the tradition and the source of the teaching.

Keeping Your Mantra a Secret

After a mantra is received, it should be kept a secret before you practice, practice and practice. There are many progressively defined steps involved in the mental practice of a mantra, and these are taught gradually. The secrecy you observe is a form of *mauna*, a practice of silence. The mantra is for internal absorption only. If it is spoken aloud, it loses its power. The mantra is to be kept within the mind. Hold it close to your bosom, close to your mind. Let it become your quiet friend when walking, or about to fall asleep, or waking up, or in the bathroom, or in the arms of your lover. That mantra becomes the very essence of your mind. Sometimes you may be conscious of it; sometimes not.

It is the duty of the initiator, the teacher, the preceptor, to lead you on, to give you the next step when you are ready. Initiation or guidance will eventually reach the inner light, the *chakras* and centres of consciousness, or the *kundalini*, when the student is ready.

The student is urged to remain in contact. The contact need not be maintained through letters, fax or e-mail, but by sitting in meditation at a fixed time daily. You will feel a very subtle and intangible connection establish. At times what happens is that when an initiator gives a mantra, the initiate continues to remain in contact for a few years and then becomes lost in life's waves and currents. A decade or so later, he feels the urge to reconnect with the teacher. He may send a letter or say, "You must have forgotten me, but my mantra has never left me." The mantra constitutes the seed from which your spirituality grows.

two

DIFFERENCE BETWEEN SUTRA AND MANTRA

Let us write *sutra* and underline *tra*. Write mantra and underline *tra.* Write the word *man*. Write the word *mna*. Write *tra* with a dash on the a, so that the *a* becomes a long vowel; this means that the vowel sound is lengthened.

What is the difference between a mantra and a *sutra*? Both these words end in the suffix *tra*. The *tra* in *sutra* and mantra is derived from the verb root *tra*, which means 'to protect', 'to confer grace'. I have a suspicion, not proved by grammarians, that this verb may have been at one time related to another Sanskrit verb root *tr*. Again, this has not been proved by grammarians, but in the yoga tradition we explain words in many ways which are not proved by the ancient grammarians. Grammarians would dispute these explanations as these are part of the oral tradition. For example, when we use the word guru, *gu* means 'darkness', *ru* means 'to protect', or 'remove from darkness' and 'protect from darkness'. There is no grammatical proof for that, but the entire yoga tradition explains guru that way. So there is a supra-grammar in the yoga tradition which is not written down anywhere. The verb root *tr* makes the *r* into a vowel like the vocalic *r* that is found in Slavonic languages. It means 'to go across', 'to swim across'. If someone is unable to swim across, then comes the act of *tra* — someone jumping in and protecting him, helping him to swim across. This is pre-grammar grammar. No Sanskrit grammarian can give this explanation. We use this verb root *tr*, to swim across, in a very definite sense in the entire yoga tradition, and is of someone conferring grace and taking us across the worldly ocean to reach the other shore. Throughout the *Upanishads* and other transcendental literature, we read of this endless ocean that we cannot swim across without a helping hand, like the other shore of a river. We speak of two kinds of sciences: *a-para* (the science of this shore) and *para* (the science of the other shore, the transcendental science). So you need a helping hand to go from *a-para* to *para*, to be able to *tr*, to get across, to swim across from the sciences, the awareness and cognition of this shore to the other shore.

Thus places of pilgrimage in India are called *tirthas,*

holy places, sacred, sanctified places in normal parlance, but actually the word means a ford, some place to get across, because the great saints and sages were the true *tirthas*, holy places. Not where they lived, but they themselves were the holy places. And you go to those *tirthas*, to those sacred places of pilgrimage because they have dwelt there. For example, the word for a class-fellow in Sanskrit is *satirthya, samana-tirthavasi,* one who lives in the same *tirtha* with you and who has the same guide to ford you across. One who lives at the same place of fording is your class-fellow. Someone who lives in the same sacred place is your classmate. So the meaning of *tra* is to swim across, to be helped across to the other shore from the world of transience to the world of transcendence.

So if we were to just jump in anyhow, without a guide, before we even reach midstream, the great guru will hear our cry: *"Trahi! Trahi!"* (Save me, protect me, guide me, lead me, please!) This is the SOS call. *Trahi* means "Help!"

We find words in Sanskrit like *tara*. Tara is the Buddhist Goddess of Compassion and she is also known in China as Quan Yin. In the Mahayana Buddhist tradition there are five aspects of Bodhisattva: the Buddha-to-be, and one of them is Avalokiteshvara, the One-Who-Looks-Down-in-Compassion, the great Lord who looks down on all beings with deep compassion. Now these Bodhisattvas, these great cosmic beings, continue their great work of *tra*, saving the beings, for aeons, in galaxies upon galaxies, and at some stage decide to go into *nirvana*. When one Avalokiteshvara decided that he was going to relinquish the universe and enter *nirvana*, a great cry arose from all the residents and denizens of these worlds: "Who will guide us now? Who will protect us? Who will look upon us with compassion?" Like the mother of countless, myriad children abandoning them and going away on a pilgrimage, this cry arose. When he heard their cries, it is said that from his left eye a single tear fell and became Goddess Tara. In Tibet she is Tara. In Korea and Japan the spelling changes a little. Tara is the one who helps us to get across, the Goddess of Compassion.

In the *Yoga Sutras* we have a word, *taraka ("Tarakam sarva-vishayam")* which means that knowledge encompasses all topics, all subjects *(pada* III, *sutra* 54*)*. It is the knowledge of all subjects which comes in a simultaneous, unsequential manner, arising from intuitive insight, while all the knowledge that arises without sequence in an instant is called *taraka*, having the same meaning: that which will lead us from transience to transcendence.

So when the seeker, the aspirant, the *sadhaka*, the disciple, tries to get across from the transient to the transcendent, or reach the other shore of pure wisdom, and starts flailing his hands in the midst of a river's fast flow, shouting, "*Trahi! Trahi! Trahi!*" (Save me! Guide me! Protect me! Please help!), then the *tirtha*, the sacred one, comes to help him ford across.

By what means does he help him to ford across? Here comes the verb root *tra,* which is the means that helps to ford us and is found in the two words: *sutra* and mantra. He protects, he guides, he helps to swim by *su*, which is actually a derivative of *siv* (to sew). A *sutra* is that which you sew with: a thread! You have *sutra* in Sanskrit and then the English word 'suture', which is derived from it. It is that which links. What does he link? He links this shore to the other shore. He, as it were, reaches out and pulls the other shore close to you. One who 'sews' you to that who links together, who connects together and thereby, *tra*, protects you. That knowledge which guides and protects you by linking you is *sutra*, by suturing together, by helping you find that thread which links all creation and all its aspects, and then links that creation to the transcendent. And that is why in ancient texts like the *Vedas* we read:

"Yo vidyat sutram vitatam
yasminn-otah praja imah,
sutram sutrasya yo vidyat
sa vidyad brahmanam mahat.
Vedaham sutram vitatam
yasminn-otah praja imah,

sutram sutrasyaham vedatho
yad brahmanam mahat."

— *Atharva-Veda* X.8.37-38

(Who knows that stretched-out thread (*sutra*) into which are beaded together all the beings who are born from the progenitor (*praja imah*); who knows the connecting thread and who knows the great knowledge of Brahman. The inquiry thus begins and then the inquiry finally ends when the disciple is able to declare: "*Vedaham sutram vitatam*" [I now know the stretched-out thread into which are linked all those beings who are the progeny of the progenitor, and I also know the hidden thread of that thread (*sutram sutrasyaham veda*), and thereby I know the great knowledge of Brahman.] So *sutra* is one way of *tra* — guiding, saving and protecting.

Mantra — with the same *tra* — has a different approach. *Mannat* means contemplation, meditation. The *sutra* process of saving grace is thus slightly different from the mantra process of saving grace. The words *sutra* and mantra are two processes of the saving grace.

And here I will tell you something about a mantra that I have not spoken of before: Let us write:

an
prana (pra + ana) and so forth:
apana,
samana,

vyana
anima
animate
animal

In all these words, there is the same verb root *an*, to be vitalised in a manner whose symptom is the breathing process. The animal only breathes, but we also write *m-an* at the beginning. Somehow there is no *manimal.* There is an animal, and I hereby coin a new word: *manimal*, which is man; animal and man. Here I'll give you another pre-grammarian grammar, and the Sanskrit grammarians will probably challenge me on this also. *An* is to breathe, from which arise words like *animal, prana,* and so on. The major sign of vitality in a living being — animal or man — is breath. It is symbolic of all the other vital signs. By observing a person's breath, you can observe the harmony, the synchrony, the healthiness and balance of all the other vital signs. Now, before *an,* add the letter *m*. Now you have *m-an*. In the mantra science, the sound *m* means the end of sound because this is the only sound that is made with the lips sealed. Also the sound *m* refers to the point of transcendence from speech into the silence of meditation, as in *AUM* where the next mantra, the hidden mantra, the secret, silent mantra, begins. In all other letters the speech is sent out. At the point of *m*, it begins to be reabsorbed. So mantra is that point where the mind and silence are added to the breath. Speech is a modification of breath, a form of the breathing process. It is the jerkiest form of breath, and that is why *yogis* take to observing silence. So when you add to your *an*, to your breathing, the silent state, you make your breath an instrument of silence through an inward process and accomplish that through m-an-tra. This is the second way of saving grace.

In the English language this verb root *man* is seen in words like *man*. I used to think that the word 'humanity' was related to it, but later found that humanity is related to humus (earth or clay) because God shaped human beings from clay, from the earth. So humanity and *man* are not related, except maybe somewhere in a pre-grammarian way. Also many other words are related to *man*, such as from Latin *mens* (meaning mind), mental, mentation and so forth.

There is another Sanskrit verb root, *mna*. In the *Oxford English Dictionary*, this verb root *mna* is recognised as being related to the verb root *man*, though the relationship is also pre-grammarian. From this verb root you get the English word, *mnemonic*. The verb root *mna* in Sanskrit means 'to mentally repeat' — first to memorise and then mentally repeat. So texts containing mantras are called *amnaya* because they are the ones that have the mnemonic content. They should be memorised, mentally repeated, and contemplated.

You may ask, "Why bother with these words?" We

say, "They are not words; they are a series of interlinked ideas." The beauty of words, especially in sacred languages, in revealed languages, is that a word contains an entire hierarchy of interlinked ideas in one puff of breath. In one puff of breath, one word links to another in a slightly different hierarchy of related ideas. So if you understand the contents of a single word, you can understand the entire hierarchy of ideas and the relationship of that ideas-capsule, called the 'word' with the next closely-related ideas-capsule. You have to find the links between the ideas-capsule and the next closely related ideas-capsule; for example, we have found the links between the ideas-capsule *sutra* and the ideas-capsule mantra, and the link between *man* and *mna* and 'mnemonic'.

The mantras were memorised and internalised. The memory process is an internalising process. Now here we come to the real difference between a *sutra* and mantra. In our study of the first chapter of the *Yoga Sutras*, we found that among the three valid proofs, the three *pramanas* recognised in the yoga tradition, the third one is called *agama*. *Agama* means "that which comes". This is the word used for any 'revealed' knowledge. This word is so fundamental that wherever the Indian culture has spread, it has used the word in that sense. For example, in countries like Indonesia and Malaysia, that are now mostly Muslim, if you go to a bookstore you will find that they will use the word *agama* for books on Islamic revealed texts!

The two religions have no connection, but the word connects them so that the *Holy Bible* would be considered also an *agama* — that which comes: *a-gacchati*.

What does "that which comes" mean? Comes from where, through what or whom, and comes to whom? From where to where, and through what or whom? It is important to understand this because the *agama* comes in two forms: *sutra* and mantra. Here we must understand the hierarchy of realities within a person:

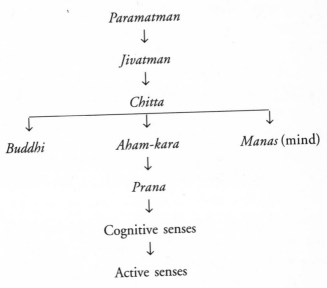

Paramatman

↓

Jivatman

↓

Chitta

↓ ↓ ↓

Buddhi — *Aham-kara* — *Manas* (mind)

Aham-kara

↓

Prana

↓

Cognitive senses

↓

Active senses

In the texts there are many different hierarchies

within a personality. There are hierarchies in the *Upanishads.* There are hierarchies within the *Gita*. There are hierarchies in the *Samkhya* and yoga texts. They all differ, depending upon the purpose of the statement. Here we take only the very basic because we are trying to understand *agama* — what comes, from where it comes. *Paramatman, Isvara*, God, the Supreme Self, the Non-individuated, the Transcendental Self has His dwelling place in *jivatman*, the individuated self. He has made for Himself a home. The *Upanishads* say: "He created and said, 'Now let me enter that which I have created and dwell within it so that it may function, so that it may be alive, so that it may be conscious'."

What is the dwelling place of *jivatman*? In which house does *jivatman*, the individuated spiritual self, live? He lives not in a glasshouse but in a crystal palace. What is that crystal palace? It is the interior face of *chitta*, the mind-field. *Chitta* is divided into three faces, three operations. Its innermost face is *buddhi*. People often translate it as 'intellect', but it is not quite what you treat as intellect. The closest term related to or expressive of the term *buddhi* is the Greek word *nous.* Do not confuse this 'higher intellect' with ordinary exterior intellectual processes. It is that crystal palace, which is cleaner, clearer, purer and more peaceful in the entire natural universe than our own mind. What you confuse as your mind is simply some mud and encrustations on the crystal. You know the mud, the humus from which humanity is made. That mud. So if a crystal falls in the mud, the nature of the crystal does not change. Someone dwelling within the crystal would hardly be aware of the mud and the encrustations because the interior of the crystal is not mud-encrusted.

So who dwells in the crystal palace, in the interior of the *buddhi*-crystal? *Jivatman*, the individuated spiritual self. The interior face of *chitta* is that *buddhi*, the crystal-clear part, the most *sattvic* place in the entire universe. That is the only place where *jiva*, the spiritual self, can live, because that is the closest that nature *(prakriti)* can come to *jiva*, to its *sattvic* face. Then comes the mind, followed by the *prana*, then the senses of cognition, and finally the active senses in the hierarchy of the constituents of a person, from the subtle to the gross.

Going back to *agama*, the revealed knowledge, 'that which comes', we may ask where it comes from? The light of knowledge, which is the very self of *Paramatman*, the Supreme Spiritual Self, sends its rays, a radiance, which passes through the *jivatman*, the individuated spiritual self, to touch the interior of the crystalline *buddhi*, the *sattvic* place. The radiance moves and filters through to reach the lower levels of the mind and moves the *prana* before becoming speech. This process of *coming* is common both to *sutra* and to mantra.

In what way, then, do *sutras* and mantras differ? Nobody gives you a *sutra* to sit and meditate and repeat, "*Atha yoganushasanam*," under your breath. That is not the way, but both are expressions of the saving grace. Now, if I want to *go* where the knowledge has come *from*, which route shall I follow? Do you know that both the English words *go* and *come* are derived from the same verb root, *gam*. So coming and going are not two separate ways: they are one and the same thing. Someone who travels from Calagary to Regina comes from here and goes there; or someone who comes from Regina to Calagary goes from there and comes here. Coming and going are like the positive and negative charges of electricity. There is no difference. There is a convention in the Sanskrit language according to which the verb root *gam* (to go) is an ideas-capsule containing three ideas in one. Wherever in the Sanskrit language a verb root of motion is used, it has three meanings — simultaneous, interwoven and inseparable, and not in sequence — *jnanam*, *gamanam* and *prapti*. All verbs of motion in the Sanskrit language are capsules of these three ideas put together, not in sequence, but simultaneously: knowing, moving and attaining. The same verbs are used for knowing; the same verbs are used for moving towards that which you know; and the same verbs are used for attaining that towards which you moved. Earlier you knew *of* it. Now, by moving towards it and attaining it, you really *know it*. So you come back full circle. Your progression starts with knowing *of* something but not yet knowing *it*.

All your progressions in life, in anything, start with knowing *of* something, and then move towards it, to gain or attain it, and thereby actually knowing it. You know at present *of* the city of New York, but you do not *know* the city of New York. So now, having heard of the city of New York *(anu-shrutya)* from someone who has been there, who has made a map of it, or has lived there, and who knows of it, and because you believe him to be a trustworthy person, you accept his word. You accept the word of a master who has been there and says that there is such a crystal palace, that there is something even beyond that because he has been there and has come from there. Language has a funny way of expressing itself.

So knowing of it from him, you move towards it, and then attain it. So the word *agama* which you have come to know of, moves towards it to attain it. Finally you attain it and thereby know it firsthand.

At present you know *of* there being a *Paramatman* (Supreme Self) because a master who has been there, who has come from there, who has taken this route down through the hierarchy of realities has spoken to you about it. Now you'll go towards it to attain it. You'll actually get there — know it personally. This entire process is included in the ideas-capsule of the word *agama*, the revealed knowledge. Through the *sutra*, you come to know of it. Through mantra you go towards it to know it. *Sutra* is the statement, the map of sages, the ones to whom the knowledge is revealed and who have drawn these maps of consciousness for us to help us link to the other shore. The maps, that have been drawn for us by the sages in their utter saving grace, tell us *of* it. Now, to go there, what route shall we follow? The route is the one that he, the revealer, had taken to come down. And what did he do? He handed us a thread, and said, "Now follow this thread." So now, the *sutra* is the process of his revelation, the ray of knowledge coming from the Supreme One into the individuated self of the great master, into his *chitta*, into his mindfield, thereby expressing it through his *prana*, which becomes his breath, his speech.

Now we have to reverse the process. Now we have to take that speech, the breath, *an*, and we have to add an *m* to it. That in English means 'to be mum', 'to be silent'. Mum is the *bija* mantra of silence. We have to take this same route and follow it back, trace it to its origin from the active sense of speech back to *prana* (convert speech into *prana* through silence), the speech that is the mantra (the word) becoming one with the breathing process; with the subtleties of *prana* vibration merging into the mentation process, *mna*, through repetition as though we were memorising or remembering it; merging that into the deeper part of the mindfield, so that all our *aham* may declare *namah* (not mine). The word *namah* in pre-grammarian grammar is 'not mine'.

At this point, the *aham* (which means 'I') gives way to *namah*, *na mama* ('not mine'), abandoning the claims of the ego, and then moving on, penetrating through the *buddhi* to the interior of the crystal palace, within which dwells *jivatman*, the individuated self. And then you penetrate further to reach *Paramatman*, the Supreme Self.

So *sutra* is the outward process of the knowledge coming to us, and mantra is the inward process of us going to the source of that knowledge.

Now all you have to do is to see the idea-capsules and link them. The similarities of sound are the links between ideas-capsules. The ancient Sanskrit grammarians studied these very, very closely. The great Sanskrit grammarian, Panini, in the 7th century BC took all the preceding grammar schools and compiled them into 4,000 *sutras*. And among those who commented on Panini was Patanjali; probably the same Patanjali, who composed the *Yoga Sutras*. Describing Panini's *sutras* as a big tome on the philosophy of grammar, he plays the devil's advocate, at one point challenging a particular *sutra* saying that it may be redundant. And then, supporting the same *sutra*, he solves the problem and concludes:

"Pramana-bhuta acharyah pavitra-panih shuchav-avakashe pran-mukha upa-vishya sutrani pra nayati sma.

Tatrashakyam varnenapy an-arthakena bhavitum kim punar iyata sutrena."

This discussion is not needed to prove the validity of this *sutra* because the validity is in the *acharya*, the great master-founder of the science himself, who, having purified himself, his limbs, sat with his eyes closed, facing the sun, and thereby revealed these *sutras*. In this revelation, not one syllable can be meaningless, let alone an entire *sutra*.

One of the three symptoms of spiritual progress is that the sense in which you use words changes. People think that you are speaking their language. You may use the same words as those used before, but your meaning has changed, as you express something entirely different and which others are not able to understand. From now on when you use the word 'come', you will use it in a different sense. When you use the word 'go', you will use it as the ideas-capsule of knowing *of* something and moving *towards* it, gaining it, and thereby *knowing* it. Knowledge is true attainment. The word then forms a circle in your mind and you understand *agama* as that which comes in both forms — *sutra* and mantra and leads you to the point from where it has come.

three

MANTRA AFTER INITIATION

Source of Mantras

Mantras are units of sound contained in a combination of syllables or words. The universe is composed of energy which contains two beams — sound and light. One does not get activated without the other, especially in the inner spiritual space. The sound units that are called mantras are not the ones that are passed on from ear to ear; that is their only physical manifestation.

In the highest state of meditation, one's spiritual self is totally one with the Divine who, being omniscient, is the source of all knowledge. The ancient Indian philosophers of language called it *shabda-Brahman*, the word that is God. Divine knowledge is available for the spiritual self to tap into.

In its trans-revelatory state, such knowledge is referred to as *para*, the transcendental speech.

As knowledge in the form of speechless speech and the wordless word flows into the individual spiritual self, it is called *pashyanti*, the Seeing One.

From here a ray of consciousness emanates and touches the mind's interior that faces the self and not the senses and the world. This interior surface is called *antahkarana*, the intuitive faculty. Here the ray of consciousness, flowing through and from the spiritual self, produces a mental vibration. The mind is stirred with awareness like that of a flash of lightning. Then, in a micro moment, which could be as subtle as 10^{57} part of a second, the entire book of the *Vedas* or all the 330 million mantras may be revealed. The experience is like a seed (*bija*) or a single dot (*bindu*) containing the details of a vast area taken from a satellite. The point has yet to be developed for the picture to manifest itself in detail. It has been described as the colours of the peacock's fan contained within the peahen's egg. This state is called *madhyama*, the middle speech.

As the knowledge rises from the depth of *buddhi* to the outward surface of the rational mind, it takes on the form of verbal thought. Words are nothing but a process of manifestation, a vibration of a lower frequency than the preceding ones. This verbal thought in the mind is named by ancient grammarians and philosophers as *vaikhari*, a divergent and harsh sound. This is only the first stage of *vaikhari*.

Now this vibration from the *buddhi*, mind and the relatively low frequency verbal thought creates a quickening in the yogi's vitality field, *prana*, which then activates the speech organs to articulate sounds as words — the final product that the disciple's ears hear in the process of transmission, initiation and teaching.

Thus, what people called the 'revealed word' is actually the veiled word at the lowest frequency of knowledge. It is veiled by layers of an individual's mind. The true unveiling occurs only in the highest meditation which is a wordless dialogue or interchange between God and one's soul. It is as though someone is in the innermost room of a cave that is a treasure house of light and as he comes out, he unravels a ball of thread. When emerging from the cave, he hands the other end of the thread to the disciple and advises him to follow the thread into the cave until the seeker of treasure reaches the internal golden womb, *hiranyagarbha*, the first and the last guru. The disciple, on receiving the sound of the mantra, uses it to gradually reach the various stations in the cave until the womb-chamber of pure consciousness is reached.

Different sound units have different effects on the mind-field and upon the *prana*-field. Therefore, they have different effects on different psycho-physiological systems within you. For this reason, to trigger a state of consciousness, one must take hold of the corresponding sound unit of a particular mantra. Then over years of practice, a student tries to trace that sound unit to its original vibration in the *prana* and from there into the mind. In the process, the mantra alters our *samskaras*, our mind states, freeing those areas which are blocked in the *prana* and in the physical centres.

What is *Japa?*

Japa is mental recitation, or better still, the remembrance, of a mantra, which gradually awakens energy vibrations in the mind-field. The practice of meditation really begins with mantra-*diksha*, the receiving of a personal mantra by initiation through a qualified teacher or preceptor in the tradition of a particular lineage; all the rest is preparation.

There are several ways of practicing *japa*. People sometimes do daily *japa*, reciting a mantra aloud. *Kirtan* or chanting is also a form of *japa*. For total beginners there is a form of *japa* which entails writing one's mantra 1,25,000 times. This is a form seldom advised in our tradition. Just having a mantra is not enough. There are stages from the beginning to the highly advanced stage in the practice of mantra. All these steps are stages in a *japa*.

The highest form of *japa* is mental *japa*, in which

one gets immersed in the silence of the mind. Here, the four phases in the practice and experience of mental *japa* are explained.

Phase One of Mental *Japa*

After one sits down in the correct posture, with the body relaxed and the diaphragmatic breathing established by doing alternate nostril breathing, one gets into the flow of the breath.

The flow of the breath may be experienced along the path of the breath from the navel to the nostrils, or it may be felt only in the nostrils, just as one does when reciting the word, the universal mantra, "*so-ham*", before receiving a mantra in initiation.

Feel the flow of the breath as cautiously as when practicing the word *so-ham* — no jerks, no breaks but a smooth flow of breath, a silent flow with no pause between the breaths. Elimination of a pause between the breaths is the most difficult part of the process, because that is the door through which external thoughts enter the mind; not through the pauses. So, exhale and immediately inhale, smoothly and slowly.

One experiences the mantra along with the feel of the breath. Some one-word mantras or *bija* mantras (seed words) pose no problem. But there are mantras that are a little longer with five letters, 12 letters or syllables or more.

Those who are not initially familiar with them have difficulty with these long mantras. So, they are advised to remain aware of the flow of the breath: let the mantra come in whatever way it comes with the breath. It may be divided over several breaths. Do not try to synchronise. In case your mantra is, "*Om namo bhagavate vasudevaya*", you may want to do *namo* while exhaling or *bhagavate* while inhaling, *vasudevaya* while exhaling, and so on. Thus you let it flow, one word merging into the next because of the breath awareness. You are reciting the mantra mentally but with the flow of breath and the touch of breath in the nostrils, or on the pathway of the breath from the navel to the nostrils, unless given some other method by the preceptor.

Phase Two of Mental *Japa*

Next, the mantra is experienced merely as a verbal thought. In the Himalayan tradition, the idea of *japa* is first to forget that the mantra is a word and to convert the word into a vibration.

The first thing one learns is to seal one's lips, the second is to still one's tongue while doing the *japa*. Third, one learns not to allow the mantra to enter other speech organs, such as the throat.

These are processes of elimination. The mantra tends to come into the speech organs the moment you lose the state of relaxation and when other thoughts intervene. Even if that happens, let the verbal thought arise at whatever speed, at whatever frequency, early and naturally for the mind. At this point, do not pay attention to the breath. If the breath has been well trained prior to initiation, it will remain diaphragmatic, smooth and devoid of jerks or breaks. If it does not, your training is incomplete and you need to keep working at it. Occasionally, you may need to observe the breath flow to ensure that you are really concentrating.

The subtle shift in *japa* comes when you stop reciting the mantra. A mantra is not your thought, not something of your doing. A mantra is the *manaso retaha*, it is the guru-mind's drop that has been planted in your mind. Through that mantra you are linked to the entire lineage, therefore the lineage will take care. So, after the first active verbal thought phase, let the mantra arise and simply observe its presence; let it *be*. If you keep using your will, doing *japa*, you will block the Divine will or guru-will working within you. So, let the mantra enter and be engaged in simply observing its presence. Awareness of the presence of mantra becomes the real *japa*.

Phase Three: Deepening the Mantra

Now, as to deepening the mantra, please understand what the mind is. At present you associate the word 'mind' only with the instrument of active thought. But the mind is not just one layer. It has many, many layers vibrating at different frequencies; thus the force-field called the 'mind' becomes subtler and subtler at deeper and deeper layers.

The common impression is that the mind articulates thoughts; however, that is not even the shallowest surface of the mind, only just a few waves of the sea hitting the beach. For a child playing on the beach, the waves hitting the beach are all he knows of the ocean. Similarly, our association with the mind's ocean is limited to these noisy waves of articulate thoughts. But the depth of the ocean is much greater. The Mariana Trench (near the Philippines) is the deepest part of the sea at a depth of 35,000 feet. If you dropped Mt. Everest there, its peak would be 6,000 feet under water. From the beach to that deepest part is quite a journey and a very deep dive.

At each subsequent level of the sea, divers know there are thermoclines — layers of water at a certain temperature, just above or below another layer of a very different temperature. As one dives deeper into the boundary line between the thermoclines, suddenly half of one's body is in a colder temperature and half in a warmer one.

So is the case when diving in the mind's ocean. At these deeper layers of the mind, the frequency of the vibration incrementally becomes higher and higher. A thought or word put into that layer vibrates at the frequency of that layer of the mind. When you dive to a deeper, higher layer of the mind, the mantra automatically is of a higher frequency. Continue to observe the level at which you find yourself and penetrate beyond that to the next layer of depth.

At all stages of meditation, observation of the state you are in is a very powerful secret — become aware of that layer of the mind, of that state. Right now you are awake; but you are not aware that you are awake. When dreaming you are not aware that you are dreaming; when asleep you are not aware that you are asleep. With awareness, these states lead towards Divine Consciousness.

Here we should again recite the mantra, remember the mantra and listen to the mantra. At each of these stages, other thoughts and images seem to come simultaneously alongside the mantra. While observing the mind very closely, I found two distinct phenomena:

- In one, the mantra and the other thoughts appear to be active simultaneously, when in reality they are actually intermittent and alternating. "Mantra; my flight time; mantra; listen to the neighbour's lawnmower; mantra; there is too much noise around here." But because the mind moves fast, we do not realise that these are intermittent and alternating. The solution is to close the gap between the breaths, and make a resolve to close the gap between mantra, mantra, mantra and mantra. One may make a resolve that for the next one minute, one will not permit any other thought but one's mantra to enter.

Try it. Right now, for one minute; just sit, relax the body, let the breath settle down, and resolve that for the next one minute there will be no thought other than your mantra. Begin now. After one minute and keeping the mantra in the mind, gently open your eyes.

In this way, you train the mind one minute at a time. In that one minute you can obtain 10 minutes of meditation if the concentration is intense and deep. It is long meditation that is required; what is needed is intense and deep meditation. Close the gap between the breaths and eliminate the pause between the mantras using one-minute and two-minute resolves at a time.

- The second phenomenon that I have observed is that the mantra and other thoughts work simultaneously. Thinking is happening at one layer of the mind while the mantra is pulsating at another. At the level of the surface, waves are hitting the beach, creating sound, but 10 feet below, it is absolutely silent. You have to shift your attention from the surface to this deeper layer. Apply the principle of observation and when you have observed the deeper layer, the waves on the surface will not end but gradually cease to matter.

At any new level, people come across unprecedented disturbances. When thoughts cease, images arise. When images cease (if you manage to overcome that phase), certain sentiments and emotions arise. Some people begin to cry; some feel like laughing; some feel angry; some become afraid; some feel sexually aroused. For each of these sentiments that arise, you need to seek the preceptor's advice because then you are at a point where you are likely to go in the wrong direction. At this stage, a lot of people say, "At this point I become frightened and come out of meditation." There are answers to these questions and a self-trained preceptor can guide you through these stages.

Phase Four of Mental *Japa*

The fourth phase in meditation should be five seconds of absolute stillness of the mind, that is if you can achieve it. Most people cannot manage more than one second of absolute stillness. One enters the chamber of silence and the mind becomes a crystal clear lake, with not a single ripple. And then from that moment of silence, one single ripple, the ripple of your mantra arises. Maintain it at that high frequency where it is barely a word before becoming a mere vibration. Then it does not take you long to recite a long mantra. *Japa* is thus understood to be a very subtle and fine art.

Different people have different experiences in that state of stillness. For some the mind feels like a vast field, or one forgets oneself, or one doesn't know how long one has been sitting in meditation as the time simply passes.

Some people may think, 'Ah, I have achieved final peace', but this stillness is not the ultimate stillness. It is a stage when the waves have stopped hitting the beach; the undercurrents of *samskaras* are still active. As stillness occurs, experiences from the subtler part of our being begin to arise. One may see a light, but not all lights are spiritual lights: it may be the light of *prana*; it may be the light of physical heat turning into an experience; it may even be something less significant than that.

Centres of Consciousness

In some cases, right at the time of the first initiation, the preceptor may asign different syllables or part syllables of the mantra to the different centres of consciousness. For example, if an initiate is given the mantra '*Namah shivaya*', she/he may be tempted to place the mantra to facilitate remembrance at five of the centres as follows:

Ascending, Exhaling		*Descending, Inhaling*	
na	perineum	*na*	eyebrows
mah	navel	*mah*	throat
shi	heart	*shi*	heart
va	throat	*va*	navel
ya	eyebrows	*ya*	perineum

It is not as staccato-like as it seems. The breath unifies the syllables and connects the *chakras*.

In most cases, however, after the mantra has been assimilated for some months or years, a specific centre of consciousness may be assigned to the initiate in which certain energy patterns and forces are visualised in a methodical manner. Or the path of *kundalini* may be introduced when the initiate's consciousness is ready for it. Many people nowadays prefer the arousal of the *kundalini*, but without the mantra and proper guidance for concentration, it could even prove harmful to one's physical and mental well-being. This is so because it is the manifestation of sound as the mantra that helps to regulate the energy flow.

There are many different ways of refining the mantra in the mind. These are taught depending on the initiate's commitment which helps him to progress and a contact is maintained between the initiate and the preceptor.

Meditation Time

Having a fixed time for meditation is the secret of success. One fixed time is a matter of *sankalpa*, determination. In addition to a fixed meditation time, tune your mind to the mantra each day whenever you can and no matter where you are for a few minutes. On the other hand, allowance is made in the texts that say, "*Mumukshunam sada kalah, strinam kalascha sarvada*" for those who are doing *japa* as seekers of liberation and for whom there is no rule about time. And ("*strinam kalascha sarvada*") for women also, there is no such rule. So there is ample freedom. This does not mean abiding by a fixed meditation time; you must stick to meditation at any cost. A certain level of *japa* should go on in the mind no matter what one is doing.

Mantra: 'Reciting' Itself

Those who have received the mantra in the yoga tradition will find that, ideally speaking, the mantra is not being *recited*; one should learn to let the mantra be. Quite often, one has to *recite* the mantra, but at other times one simply invites, invokes the presence, lets the mantra arise by itself and continue in the mind. Many times, even that invocation, that invitation, is not necessary. Often one finds, on waking up at night, that the mantra is going on: one is in the bathroom and the mantra goes on; or one is in the embrace of one's spouse and the mantra continues.

Simply learn to listen to the mantra within and become absorbed in listening.

The mantra in the yoga tradition is called a *bija* (seed); a seed is implanted in the mind, that is, a tiny particle of the guru's mind is implanted into the disciple's mind. Therefore, it has its own movement. Even if you do not recite your mantra six years from now, or 10 years from now, somewhere it is bound to come up. It is said in the yoga tradition that the mantra given to you goes with you even through death. In our teaching of the art of dying, we prefer to train people for the day when they will leave the body as the mantra accompanies them on their passage to death.

Progression in Purification

The mantra is for penetrating through the veils and curtains of *samskaras*, for countering the existing *samskaras*, and for preventing the formation of new, undesirable *samskaras*.

Samskaras are impressions of our past actions stored in the unconscious mind.

Or, in the language of the *Yoga Sutras* of Patanjali, to prevent the *klishta vrittis* (afflicted *vrittis*) from arising, and to develop and maintain one single *aklishta vritti* (unafflicted *vritti*), so that *shuddhi*, *buddhi*, *siddhi* and *mukti* may occur.

Shuddhi is purification; *buddhi*, awakening of pure and *sattvic* awareness; *siddhi*, fulfilment of the purpose of *japa* and *mukti* is freedom.

We have to penetrate through the curtain of *samskaras*, the five *koshas* or sheaths of the body, *prana*, mind, knowledge and bliss; through the three bodies — gross, subtle, causal; to the interior-most part of the *buddhi* beyond which the mantra does not reach and at which point the mantra is dropped.

Use of the *Mala*

Different types of *malas* (necklaces) are needed for reciting different mantras. One may be advised to wear a particular *mala* all the time and use a different kind of *mala* for reciting the mantra. All this is between the student and the preceptor.

Big bead *malas* slow you down. By the time you cross from one side of the hill to the other, two seconds would have passed. The big bead *malas* can be worn for decorative purposes but for doing *japa*, small beads with a little knot in between, are used.

Do you need to use the *mala*? There are two different aspects to *japa*, each of which has its own purpose. One often needs to go through a period of discipline with the *mala*: "I shall do so many repetitions." In practice, do a part of the *japa* with the *mala*, so that basic discipline is maintained and once a habit is formed, put the *mala* aside and go into meditation. Visualising the pathways to subtler depths, put aside the *mala* and enter deeper, deeper, and deeper into the mind.

Purash-charanas

I often advise the new initiates to undertake a *purash-charana* immediately after initiation. The word *purash-charana* means 'a foot forward', which entails undertaking a special observance. A beginning of *purash-charana*, for example, would entail a repetition of the mantra 1,25,000 times on the *mala*. Then the mantra becomes a habit and is absorbed by the mind. Knowing the number of minutes it takes to complete one *mala* of your mantra, and how many minutes are available daily, you can decide on the number of sessions required in the day. One session should be at your fixed time while the hours of the other sessions may vary.

On completing 1,25,000 repetitions of the mantra, get in touch with your preceptor, who will advise you to either observe the same again, or do it differently. At a certain point of your progress, the preceptor may assign:

- special modes of breathing with the mantra;
- *chakras* or centres of consciousness to meditate upon; and
- certain internal visualisations, or internal rituals.

He may assign any of the five pillars of *sadhana:*

- stillness
- celibacy
- silence
- fasting
- conquest of sleep to a lesser or greater degree

For guidance, you have to remain in touch with your preceptor. Try to put aside three days, five days, seven days, 10 days, or a month every year to forget the world and enjoy the freedom of a retreat for an intensive practice of the mantra.

Other Aspects of Deep Mantra Meditation

When the body is tired, the mind becomes sluggish because the mind draws part of its energy from *prana*. When the *prana* moves at a lower frequency or in erratic patterns, the mind also moves slowly and erratically. Therefore it is important for one who is keenly interested in developing his or her *sadhana* to be at rest. Resting not only means the required amount of sleep; it also means using conscious rest as in *shavasana* practice which eventually leads to the practice of *yoga-nidra*. To be rested means that after the day's hectic activities, one must gradually train the mind to rest so that the activity does not draw out more energy of the body than is absolutely required for the task undertaken. Silence is most restful.

Resting by itself is not enough. Physical yoga practices activate *prana* and align and harmonise the *prana* flow, taking it to higher frequencies. Once you have activated the *prana* through *hatha yoga*, go through a relaxation exercise, and other *shavasana* practices. After this, sit up and do *nadi-shodhanam*, alternate nostril breathing, to balance the left- and right-flowing energies.

One has to train oneself in many directions of life. All the *yamas* and *niyamas* (*ahimsa*, detachment and so on) are guidelines for emotional purification. Otherwise, our emotions produce random thoughts, slow down the mind and exhaust the body. Emotional purification is an entirely different *sadhana* to go along with *japa sadhana.* The *sadhana* of emotional purification is a life-long endeavour of self-observation and self-refinement — *atma-samskara, atma-shuddhi, manah-shuddhi.* Emotions are where people get stuck, where the progress in meditation gets blocked. But then, the more *japa* you do, the more the emotions begin to purify slowly, and vice versa.

What to Do with Previous Mantras

The question often asked, before or after a mantra initiation, is, "What do I do with the mantras I have previously received?"

Both in the West and in India people seek many initiations. In the West people simply like to experiment with this mantra or that mantra, with this teacher or that teacher. It is a common practice to experiment. In India people feel that it would add to their sanctity or holiness if they accumulate initiation. To both, the initiates of the West and East, our advice is that having many mantras is like having multiple partners. The mind becomes divided. When the purpose of the mantra is to make the mind still, reciting many mantras is not helpful.

People in India are highly ritualistic, using elaborate *pujas* and so forth entailing many rituals, many mantras and many prayers. These are all exterior acts. In many *tantric* works, besides the *kriya pada* and *charya pada*, the chapters on rules of rituals and on daily disciplines of life, there is often a chapter on *yoga pada,* the interior part of observance. Very few people are familiar or conversant with the interior part of a mantra. So we describe the mantra practice here. People tend to satisfy themselves only through exterior acts. In churches and synagogues in the West, the external rituals, prayers and hymns satisfy devotees the same way as they do the temple-going devotees in India. The cultural milieu is different but the idea is the same.

In India, mantras are given or received or recited in many different ways:

- As already stated, mantras are a part of external rituals. The priest often gives mantras, for example, to the twice-born, the *Gayatri* mantra is given at a certain age by the priest-preceptor. People practice the *Gayatri* mantra as much as possible throughout their lives.
- Sometimes people overseas decide to embark on some aspect of spiritual life, and approach their priest or astrologer for a mantra. How do the priests and astrologers select the mantras? In the following ways:
    - There is *anka vidya*, the science of numerology, which is very ancient in India and in which the numbers have a close association with the letters of the alphabet. This tradition is

found also among the Jews, who have done an entire analysis of the Hebrew *Bible* to find, say, prophetic codes and numerological interpretations of syllables. The mantra may be matched numerologically to one's name or birthdate.

- In India, unlike the present-day West, astrology is not merely a science of prediction. No astrologer is consulted if he is unable to suggest a preventive measure to change existent circumstances, because with every astrological prediction, forces can be moved around. So if *A* is in a bad place, the astrologer tells him the appropriate mantra and the rituals which can be performed along with it. One's *rashi*, the sign of the Zodiac, determines which forces need to be brought into play to ward off the ill effects of the *rashi*, or to enhance the good effects of another one.
- Quite often, priests who are not bound to a particular religious denomination, may ask an initiate who his *ishta devata* is, that is, his favourite form of the deity. Some speak of their family deity; others speak of the personal deity they are most drawn to. By the word 'deity' we mean a form of Divinity, the manifestation

to which we are attracted, either due to family tradition or personal choice. Based on their answers, a mantra is given.

- Then there are certain mantras that are handed down over generations as part of the family tradition. The mantra is passed on from a father to his son, from a mother to her daughter. Sometimes the daughter-in-law receives a mantra from the mother-in-law upon marriage. Just as the son is a continuity of the father, the daughter-in-law is a continuity of the mother-in-law. A daughter does not continue the parental family, but continues the family she is married into. Just as upon marriage, the bride often receives a new name, many women receive a mantra from their mothers-in-law, or from the priests of their new families.
- There are also *sampradaya* mantras signifying various religious denominations within which people receive their respective mantras. This is illustrated in the story of Ramanuja, who received a mantra from Nambi. The *acharya* said, "The mantra should be kept a secret," but Ramanuja went to the rooftop and shouted the mantra to the whole world, "*Aum namo bhagavate vasudevaya*", 'I have received such a great treasure'.

The *acharya* was angry, "I told you, it was supposed to be kept a secret."

Ramanuja said "I was so overjoyed to receive such a treasure that I wanted to share the treasure with everybody."

So everybody in this tradition has the same mantra, or there is the Chaitanya Mahaprabhu tradition in which everyone receives the same mantra. It's like a Hindu getting converted to Christianity to receive the Lord's prayer.

Now, let us say that you have received your *sampradaya* mantra — a mantra of your particular religious denomination and ritually you recite all the other mantras as well. How do these mantras differ from the tradition of the *yogis*? In each of these traditions, there is a certain spiritual force present. There is no question about it, except that the focus is more on the form of the deity to which the individual is drawn through that mantra.

In the *yogic* tradition, a person authorised to initiate uses an intuitive process to assign mantras. Those who are authorised to give initiation, mantra-*diksha*, are taught to arrive at a mental state where intuition alone plays a major role in receiving the mantra to be given to the initiate. The aim is to reduce mental conflict as much as possible and unify the mind through concentration. The mantra is not meant for performing rituals; it is for inward absorption only. It is for penetrating the veils of the five *koshas* and of the three bodies until the mantra reaches a point where, as the *Shiva Sutras* say, "The entire mind becomes the mantra." Beyond that when one reaches the state of *a-manaska-yoga*; not only is the mantra left behind, the mind too is left behind.

Now arises the question: "What do I do with the mantras I have received before?" The mantra received in the *yogic* tradition, as I have said earlier, is for inward absorption only. If you have a denominational (*sampradaya*) or family mantra and you perform your external worship, then carry on your worship with the mantra appropriate for that aspect of Divinity. What you do with your *sampradaya* mantra, or your family mantra, or the one given by the mother-in-law to the daughter-in-law, involves a few recitations. When you see a beautiful piece of jewellery, you do not throw away your old jewellery. You keep it alongside the new piece. These mantras are not mantras for your regular meditation practice; they serve different purposes to keep your link with your *sampradaya*, your denomination, to keep your family tradition going and help you perform worship and *pujas*.

Therefore, if you have other mantras in addition to the regular guru-mantra, which is received in *yogic* initiation, perhaps even the new mantra given by your preceptor, repeat one to three times all your mantras to remember and honour them. Do five, do 11 or you may end your mediation with the same recitation again. But let your major work during meditation and throughout the day be with your personal guru-mantra. In the *yogic* tradition you should learn to differentiate between what people do with the mantras overtly and what is the covert purpose of the mantra in meditation.

How to Recite Fast the Long Mantras

Often there are questions about the mind's ability to do *japa* of the long mantras effectively when a person has limited time. Many people take about half an hour to complete one round of the *mala* for performing *mrityunjaya* mantra, for example, or for the *Gayatri* mantra. At this speed, if a *purash-charana* is undertaken, the observance of a *japa* with 1,25,000 repetitions plus 20 per cent of the number will take years. So how can these long mantras be tackled while saving time?

Principle of *Ardha-matra*: Half a *Mora* Again and Again

There is a principle called *ardha-matra* or half a *mora*. A *mora* is the time taken to pronounce a short vowel. One learns to pronounce a *mora* in half the time. Here we are not speaking of articulation or recitation of it with the mouth, or murmuring it silently through the speech organs. Many people perform silent *japa*, permitting it to reach the speech organs, throat, larynx or a moving tongue, even if the lips are sealed. Reciting the mantra too fast will only increase tension and not serve the purpose of entering deep meditation.

The principle of *ardha-matra* can be understood only if we know the nature of the mind as explained above, remembering that the mind is not just made up of one layer. It has many layers vibrating at different frequencies and this force-field called the 'mind' becomes more and more subtle at the deeper layers of the mind. At these layers the frequency of the mind's vibration incrementally becomes higher and higher. It is taught in the *Tantras* that the mantra may be refined nine times thus:

1/2
1/4
1/8
1/16
1/32
1/64
1/128
1/256
1/512

Even in the subtle point of life-force and consciousness in the *sahasrara chakra*, in the highest centre of the 1,000 rays, there are nine levels within that *bindu* itself. All that is part of the *ardha-matra* system. We start with the time taken to pronounce, no, to mentally remember a short vowel, the *mora*, and then reduce it by half, and then half of that and so on till we reach a higher and higher frequency.

Let a Quiet Resolve Arise in the Mind

When sitting for meditation, let there arise a *sankalpa* in your mind, a quiet resolve and not a loud determination. A resolve like the sure and quiet one a person feels when a person is in love. Just realise this something within, that way. At each stage, each state, each phase of mediation, renew that resolve. Don't make that resolve for the next half hour, but for the next minute. Don't say, "I shall not permit", but rather, say gently, "For the next minute, there shall not arise any intruding [sic] thoughts; I shall experience only the even flow of my breath." Just as we have learned to close the gaps in our breathing process through a one-minute practice, make a quiet resolve to have no intrusive thoughts for one minute, starting from now.

How did that minute pass? Resolve that for the next one minute no intrusive thoughts will enter except for the presence of your shorter personal mantra coming like a thought-wave repeating itself; a wave into which there will be no intrusive thoughts for the next minute. You will only feel the flow of your breath in your nostrils and the presence of your mantra.

Now for maintaining this state of mind, repeat the following *Gayatri* mantra twice:

"Om bhur buvah svah
tat savitur varenyam
bhargo devasya dhimahi
dhiyo yo nah prachodayat."

Return to the same state of mind that you were in during the one-minute following the resolve; now resolve that during the two repetitions of the thought-wave called the *Gayatri*, there will be no interrupting thoughts. Now begin. That was one minute. In that one minute, recite the *Gayatri* mantra 21 times or more because you enter a higher frequency deep in the mind.

Now attempt to recite the long mantra, keeping the words in tune with the breath and dividing the mantra over several breaths. Recite the fragment "*Om bhur buvah svah*", and see how long it takes. Initially recite the fragment in one exhalation as many times as possible in that one exhalation. Similarly, try on your own with the second fragment, "*Tat savitur varenyam*", and then the third segment, "*Bhargo devasya dhimahi*", then the fourth "*Dhiyo yo nah prachodayat*". Recite segment by segment with the same resolve as made earlier with the shorter mantra, permitting no interrupting thoughts. It is these thoughts that take you to the lower frequency, the shallower level of the mind. By intruding between mantra and mantra, they slow down your *japa*. So eliminating these thoughts, recall the state you experienced when you reached the slightly higher frequency level for one minute, and keep referring to it. Gradually increase the period of resolve to two minutes and then three minutes and so on.

Let the entire mantra flash as a single unit.

Now relax completely. Let your breath settle down and permit your personal mantra to come to your mind. Do not let the mantra enter word for word or syllable by syllable. Let the entire mantra flash as a single unit, as though your mind is a clear sky with one single star flashing bright. Now let the first segment of the *Gayatri* mantra flash in the same way; then the second segment, followed by the third and then the fourth before the entire segment is completed as a single unit.

Now recall the first and second segments together. Let the third and fourth segments flash as a thought-wave. Remain there.

Now recite the entire mantra. Gradually the practice will improve as the mind learns to enter higher frequency levels.

Let the Mind Observe the Mind

There is one more secret for reaching deep meditation and learning to perform the long mantra. Observe the mind. Let your mind feel the presence of the mantra. The part of the mind that is employed to experience the thought-wave is a small fragment of the mind. The rest of the mind wanders off and this should be employed till the doer and the observer merge. Those who have been initiated into a *chakra* will find a certain vibration in that *chakra* and learn to merge their consciousness. Sit in grace and surrender. Not by your effort alone can you reach total purification, enlightenment. Your effort only purifies the vessel. Surrender your body, *prana* and mind so that the guru-spirit may enter and the guru-mind may touch your mind, making it a seat for meditation.

However, you may not succeed in the practice simply by reading about the technique described above. Seek out a qualified preceptor who will help in transmission of the vibration and open some of the interior doorways in a personal or small group session. What we have tried with the *Gayatri* mantra also works for the *mrityunjaya* mantra or any other long mantra given to you.

May you delve into the deepest layer of the mind and beyond. God bless you, *Om*.

Two-Mantra Meditation Practices

Practice One: Meditation with Mantra

- Sit with your head, neck and trunk straight; your spine held erect.
- Withdraw your mind from all other places and be aware only of the place where you are sitting.

- Withdraw your mind from all other spaces and be aware only of the space your body occupies from head to toe. Be aware of yourself from head to toe.
- Withdraw your mind from all other times to be aware of this moment in time. Be here and now in your awareness.
- Relax your forehead, your eyebrows and eyes, your nostrils, cheeks, the jaw, the corners of your mouth, the chin, your neck, shoulders, upper arms, lower arms, your hands, your fingers, and your fingertips. Now breathe in, feeling your breath flow all the way to your fingertips.
- Relax your fingertips, your fingers, your hands, lower arms, upper arms, shoulders, chest, and your cardiac region. Gently exhale and inhale, slowly and smoothly.
- Relax your stomach, your navel, your abdomen, your thighs, your calf muscles, your feet and your toes. Breathe in, allowing your breath to flow through your whole body, from top to toe gently, slowly and smoothly.
- Relax your toes, your feet, your ankles, your calf muscles, your knees, your thighs, your abdomen, your navel, your stomach, your cardiac region, your chest, your shoulders, your upper arms, your elbows, your lower arms, your wrists, your hands,

your fingers and your fingertips. Holding your neck straight, relax your neck muscles, your chin, your jaw and the corners of your mouth, cheeks, nostrils, eyes and eyebrows, forehead and the seat of your mind. Gently exhale and inhale, allowing your breath to flow through your whole body, from top to toe and toe to top, gently, slowly and smoothly.

- Observe the gentle rise and fall of your stomach and the diaphragm muscles. Observe how that area gently relaxes as you inhale, and see it contract as you exhale. Observe the movement with the gentle rhythm of your breathing.
- Establish diaphragmatic breathing.
- Let your mantra come to your mind easily, naturally and comfortably. Exhaling and inhaling, let your mantra come many times in your breath. If it synchronises with your breath, let it synchronise, or simply let the mind remember the mantra, easily, naturally and comfortably. Feel the diaphragmatic breathing.
- Feel the flow and touch of your breath in your nostrils, breathing slowly, gently and smoothly. There should be no break in your breath, no jerks, no sound. Continue to feel the touch of your breath in the nostril. Maintain the mantra in whatever way it comes easily, in whatever way it adjusts to

your breathing, any number of times in your breath, or divided over several breaths. Exhale and inhale.

- If your mind begins to wander, straighten your spine and your neck. Relax your abdomen, stomach, chest and shoulders. Relax your jaw and forehead. Re-establish diaphragmatic breathing.
- Again feel the flow and touch of the breath in the nostrils. Maintain the mantra in whatever way it adjusts to your breathing, as many number of times as possible in your breath.
- Now you may ignore your breathing. Let your mantra enter your mind in whatever way it wants, naturally and comfortably. Let the mind remember the mantra, over and over again.
- Observe your mind doing so.
- Do not turn away from your mantra. Relax and let the mind remember the mantra over and over again.
- Now cease all effort. Abandon all endeavour. Let there be a quietness, stillness and silence in the mind.
- In this restful silence, let your mantra arise, pulsating further and further.
- Again feel the flow and touch of your breath in your nostrils, as though your breath and the mantra are a quiet stream flowing though your pool of silence.
- Observe the flow of your breath and the presence of the mantra.

- Gently, without losing touch with your breath and the mantra, slowly cup your eyes with your palms. Remaining inwardly tuned, gently open your eyes to your palms. Continue to enjoy the feeling of calmness before bringing your hands down.
- God bless you.

Practice Two: One-minute Meditation with Mantra

- First centre your body from the nose, using the breath. Then establish diaphragmatic breath.
- Resolve for one or two minutes to not allow any other thought to enter the mind while maintaining the prescribed concentration.
- Feel the breath while breathing with your whole body — from the crown to the feet for one minute.
- Feel the breath in the navel centre for one minute.
- Feel the breath flowing in the channel between the navel and the centre at the base of the nostrils for one minute.
- Do *nadi-shodhanam*.
- Feel the breath in the active nostril for one minute.
- Feel the breath in the passive nostril for one minute.
- Feel the breath flow through both nostrils for two minutes.
- Feel the breath flow through the channel between the centre of the base of the nostrils and the centre

between the eyebrows (*sushumna* breathing) for two minutes.

- Do *sushumna* breathing while repeating the mantra in your mind for two minutes.
- Sense only the mantra in your *ajna* (eyebrow) centre for two minutes.
- Be aware of complete silence for a quarter of a minute.
- Feel the breath flow through both nostrils with the mantra for one minute.
- Open your eyes while maintaining awareness of breath and hearing the mantra for one minute.
- Open your eyes while maintaining breath awareness and hearing the mantra for one minute.
- Move the body, stretch and relax.

four

SPECIAL MANTRAS

Mantras may be recited with a motive or without one. The motives are *sa-kama*, literal meaning being 'with desire', for fruit and result. Without motives mantras are *nish-kama*, without desire, only to gain purification leading to liberation. *Sa-kama* is of two kinds: (1) fulfil a personal desire, such as, change in the nature of one's husband or riches, (2) a subtler kind is "I want to live a life of prayer, worship [or service], but practical obstacles come in the way" or "I cannot pray or serve because my husband won't let me, as he is jealous". To correct such situations, the practice is the same as the first, but with an ultimate desire or *sa-kama*. Here the *sa-kama* desire is to pave the way for the *nish-kama* goal. Even the desire for liberation may be dropped, and the mantra may be practiced *guru-prity-artham,* for the guru's satisfaction and to receive grace.

Sa-kama may be done for specific purposes, such as to ward off or heal an illness, to prevent accidents, to prolong life, to alleviate financial problems, to achieve a specific goal such as to be able to buy a house, or capture power, or improve an organisation, or regain friendship, or eliminate animosity towards self, and so on and so forth.

Sa-kama may be undertaken (a) for the purpose of self-purification and liberation only, or (b) to obtain a desired result, or (3) to attain the *siddhi* in that mantra. The formula of 'the number of syllables multiplied by hundred thousand plus 20 per cent' is definitely efficacious to achieve the *siddhi*. Now one has the power inherent in the mantra and is able to use the mantra with just one or three or a minimum number of remembrances to attain the desired result for oneself or for one's students or seekers.

Quite often a guru in his grace passes on the power of the mantra to a disciple without the latter resorting to these recitations. I recall a day in 1972 when I was driving my Gurudeva along Hennepin Avenue, Minneapolis. I complained, "You have great disciples sitting in the Himalayas doing all the *tapasya*, and here I am running around American cities. How will I make any progress?"

My guru said, ever so compassionately, "Why do you need to do that, when I have done it all? I have already passed on to you the benefits of 10,000,000 *Gayatri* mantras. Have you not felt it?"

"Yes, indeed I have felt it," I replied.

I have heard similar stories from other fellow disciples.

According to our tradition, we advise people to undertake special *anushthanas* (observances) of many repetitions of special mantras from time to time and for specific periods. Normally, these have been in units of 1,25,000 plus 20 per cent. Actually, these are for beginners. To determine a full *purash-charana*, the principle is: count the number of syllables in a given mantra (for example, the *Gayatri* has 24 syllables), and recite it a hundred thousand times. Thus a complete observance of the *Gayatri* mantra will entail 2,400,000 mental recitations, plus 10 or 20 per cent — the reason for this will become clear below.

How long would this take? Let us first look into the amount of time needed for 1,25,000 recitations plus 20 per cent; that is 1,500 *malas*. Calculate how long it takes one to complete one *mala* of the given mantra. Some beginners manage only, say, one *mala* per 10 minutes. Allowing for distractions, let it be an average of five *malas* per hour. By calculating how many hours a day one can sit and dividing the time into several sessions, one can arrive at the number of days required. Let us say that one sits twice a day for an hour each; so, 10 *malas* per day for 150 days equal five months.

In ancient times, and for those who today manage to

lead the life of *sadhana*, a *purash-charana* of 1,25,000 might be completed in the shortest possible time; normally not more than three months for the lazy, full-time *sadhaka*. For the likes of us who have households or *ashrams* to think about, it is best not to set a time limit. In my present circumstances, it takes two months to complete 1,25,000 fire offerings. Setting a time limit causes unnecessary stress and anxiety because external circumstances intervene: a child may fall sick, a wedding has to be attended, an unexpected visitor from somewhere near the North Pole drops in at the *ashram* with a dire spiritual need and then one has to rush through the *japa* to complete it on time. This is indeed a distraction. One may simply express the desire that 'I would like to complete it in such and such time; God and guru, please bless me,' and then do one's best.

If one has a lot of time and inclination, can one complete the recitation in a very short time? Unless you are a very highly accomplished *sadhaka*, try not to attempt it this way. The 'deities', the conscious powers inherent in the mantras, do not wish to be rushed. Too many adjustments all at once may bring intense results that you are not ready for. Therefore, the middle path is the best.

If one is serious about one's spiritual life, or wants to obtain any other result, one should cut out other distractions, like social parties, videos, reading stories and so forth. As the *japa* proceeds, the need for sleep gets naturally reduced. It can be further reduced through the practice of *yoga-nidra*. One can, with such adjustments in life, find time to sit three-and-a-half hours per day as follows:

One hour in the morning;
half an hour after coming from work;
two hours (with a break in between) at night.

Few have undertaken the full 2,400,000 *Gayatri* mantras or 3,200,000 *mrityunjaya* mantras (which have 32 syllables) plus 20 per cent. These are the individuals who have no special worldly responsibilities, or are retired and have made their five-year spiritual plans with care. They are people with a strong determination. Those few who have undertaken such an observance try to continue with varying degrees of diligence under guidance. The preceptor prays for their successful conclusion. Those who have completed such an observance have the charisma to attract many seekers and draw students to themselves without effort.

By keeping to the same kind of calculations as above, one may complete such an ambitious *purash-charana* or *Gayatri* mantra or *mrityunjaya* mantra or any such long mantra, in three to five years. Instead of going to a business office, one goes to God's office to devote the requisite hours for meditation.

If one feels too overwhelmed by the idea of so many

millions (it is not currency notes but mantras!), one may recite it piecemeal. Recite 25,000 at a time, pause a while, start the same number again, and thus keep repeating the same short observance till you are a multi-millionaire. It's perhaps easier on the mind that way.

It is quite normal that during the course of a *purashcharana* you experience unexpected upheavals, obstacles, unwelcome changes. This is like homeopathic medicine. Some *karmas* and *samskaras* that would fructify slowly over a lifetime, or even over the next five years, reach the surface in a short time. Do not give up in the middle, saying; "Oh, this mantra is very harmful; my teacher does not know his science and has put me in trouble." No, do not abandon the undertaking. It is the phase of dissolution before creation; a readjustment. Once the crisis passes, you will see a fresh and more beautiful start — the *karma* has been paid off.

This entire process is based on the principle of *prayashchitta*, expiation; voluntary paying off of the *karma*. In fact, whenever one realises that one has transgressed a universal law or committed a 'sin' by hurting someone, one may undertake an expiation which has the effect of self-purification. Some expiate such transgressions by giving an anonymous donation, or by serving the elderly for a time, or by going on a pilgrimage, or fast, or observing a period of silence. In the Sikh tradition, one may be required to clean the shoes of all those who enter the temple, or sweep the floors of the temple for a specific number of days. But the most purifying form is *japa*.

Now, in the course of such an observance, one's mind will pass through many different stages, moods and feelings — ennui, boredom, fatigue, bursts of energy and enthusiasm, moments of unprecedented peace, an urge to quit. The *samskaras* appear on the surface and subside. Do not struggle; do not abandon. Take to the middle path. Forgive yourself. Accept yourself. Remain determined to complete it, even if on some days your tiredness tells you to perform no more than one *mala* that day; keep doing so. The mood will pass and you will be happy. When one is tired, the going is always slower; when one is rested, the progress is faster. Allow yourself periods of rest. It all requires arranging your time-table. Gently do it.

Eating *sattvic* food is important. The priests, who undertake such performances for others, often require a special allowance of extra milk and some *ghee* daily.

To nourish themselves, some people in India often take hot milk boiled with ground almonds. Five almonds are soaked overnight, skinned in the morning, ground and eaten with a glass of milk. Some add a little *ghee* to the hot milk. For those in the West, half a teaspoon (for the hardy Punjabis, it is a tablespoon!) of *ghee* in milk will do (but not if you have a heart problem or are overweight) together with two or three black peppercorns. It is a very wise balancing act. At night one may take a glass of milk with saffron cooked in it. Ask any Indian woman how exactly it is done. It is the gentlest soporific.

Now, back to the application of the practice of the mantra.

A master may be able to use a mantra once, thereby making the necessary adjustments in the subtle world, to achieve a desired goal. He will do so only if the recipients of grace gain spiritual benefits or are enabled to serve others. Not everyone walking down the street can be helped unless she/he is interested to serve or achieve a spiritual goal.

A teacher-priest, initiated in the yoga tradition and who is not yet a master, may have to recite the mantra a certain number of times to achieve the desired goal. A householder leading a worldly life may have to do it even longer. His/her mantra will be more effective if he/she gets initiated into it by a qualified initiator in yoga before starting the long *japa* practice. One may also employ a priest of *sattvic* temperament to sit daily and perform the *japa* for the officiant's (*yajamana's*) benefit. But the *yajamana* needs to take care of such a priest who has to sit practically full time. I have employed such priests in the last one year to achieve certain objectives as I did not have time to do the *japa* myself. I was engaged in trying to accomplish a number of projects for the mission as well as for my beloved students. The cost of that many fire offerings can be calculated. Nowadays people are generous with the cost of buying a new sofa, but often do not wish to support keepers of traditions. Please remember that selflessness alone invokes grace.

If one wants it done this way, it is advisable to perform some *malas* oneself at the same time, at least 10 per cent.

If 1,25,000 *japas* are done without the fire offerings, then 10 per cent more with fire offerings, or 20 per cent more without any fire offerings need to be done. In other words, a 1,25,000 *purash-charana* ends up consisting of 1,50,000 repetitions.

As said earlier, one needs to calculate how long it takes to do one round of the *mala*, how many hours a day one can sit, and then calculate the time taken to complete the practice. 150,000 repetitions of *japa* mean 1,500 *malas*.

There is always a concern among beginners about the time required to chant long mantras. As time passes, one masters the special art of reciting the mantra faster and less time is required. It has nothing to do with moving the tongue, but has more to do with entering the higher frequency layers of the mind. As one delves deeper, the speed automatically improves. One may choose to sit with a qualified preceptor to learn this art fully.

It is advisable to set one fixed time in the day to sit and meditate. One may have other sessions in the day at flexible times or have as many brief or extended sessions as one desires, but not between 12 to 3 o' clock in the day or at night.

Even if one is ill, or travelling, or busy with sick children, one should sit at a fixed time at least for one *mala*. The daily link must be maintained. If the mind is unsettled during that one *mala*, it is best not to count it in the final calculations. Better to do more than to lose some. Be greedy as you would be with money due to you from a tax refund. Try to become a millionaire in mantra recitation.

Special *purash-charana* practice counts only if it is done by sitting down. One does not, unlike one's guru-mantra (*mula*-mantra), practice the special ones while walking about, etc.

The special practice begins with a *sankalpa*, a special resolve regarding the place, time, person and motive. A set of formulae are recited for the *sankalpa*, a copy of which, in brief English paraphrase from Sanskrit, is appended herewith.

In the *sankalpa* come the subtleties of the motives and purpose. I may give someone the same *maha-mrityunjaya* mantra as a prayer for health and as a prayer for spiritual liberation. Or the two objectives may be combined with the thought that if the practicant (*sadhaka*) completes the practice and is freed of his illness, he will dedicate himself to liberation. Or, that since he is giving up other desires in favour of liberation, his past selfish *karmas* will be reduced and he will, incidentally, be cured of the disease while achieving liberation. To someone else I give a mantra which combines the effect of (a) curing a chronic illness and (b) giving oneself to the service of others with the life span thus enhanced. In such a case, the enhancement of life span will not occur unless one discovers such dedication in oneself.

One has to decide by what mode one wants to solve a problem. Take the case of a litigation going on for years as filed by some vindictive people against someone innocent. The victim needs to decide whether (a) he/she wants to win the case, or (b) does he/she want to win the person over by bringing changes in the character of the perpetrator? The latter will take a longer time than the former but the change will be more deep-rooted. On the other hand, if one wants to win over someone who is temporarily upset or angry, the change will be quicker.

Again, I have found that if you wish to solve the problem by bringing a change in the character of the other person, such a change is often a temporary one. It will solve your immediate problem by evoking *saumanasyata*, good mindedness, eupsychea. But the force of *samskaras* is strong and people revert to their basic nature in other relationships. I have to keep repeating the same experiment — do the same *japa* again next year, and so on until the *samskara* is completely wiped out. This is what gurus do to change us. But, then, gurus have *astras*, missiles, while we have only the mantra at *vaikhari*, or verbal level, or at most at *madhyama*, the mental thought level, and cannot take full responsibility for all our students. There are not enough months in a year to accomplish everything.

When doing the *japa* to change a person or a situation, do not say anything to him. Be indifferent to all his external acts. Meet politely; make no special overtures at this time. It is best to tell no one else either. A mantra implies secret. Keep it a secret. Do not even inquire if there is any change in that person? Do not hold on to anxiety; merely surrender.

But only *japa* will not do. Your own acts should match the purification you desire in the other. You are trying to change an 'enemy' into a friend by making him a more *saumya* person, one with moonlike characteristics. Then, you must be perfect in your own *maitri bhavana* (*Yoga Sutra* I.33). Do not pray for a change in him while your mind recounts all the injustices he has done to you. Without such pure *japa,* you will not accomplish your purpose. For this *maitri bhavana*, not only do you need to keep your mind pure but also do things beneficial to the other person secretly, or describe that person's virtues to others and mean it. Slowly you will learn to refine the art of making your *japa* more and more effective.

In one case I gave someone a mantra to help him succeed in a difficult sutuation. The practicant had a lot of anger against somebody and the thoughts of that constantly intervened in the *japa*. The adverse effects began to tell not on the situation that was meant to be corrected but rather on the person for whom there was anger in the practicant's mind. I had to tell the practicant to stop reciting the mantra and get it completed by some priests (and meet the expenses) to mend the situation. So, a preceptor has to be on the lookout for such situations constantly, otherwise it would be tantamount to committing murder. Do you still want to be a guru?

Do not try to rectify irreversible situations. There is no point in trying to recite the *mrityunjaya* mantra if one knows that the illness is terminal. Yes, do it or have it done, but as a prayer for the liberation of the soul and for the dying person's peace of mind, but not for a cure. In case of a terminal illness, I give the *shatakshara Gayatri* for the person's peace of mind. If the person cannot do *japa*, I simply let him listen to the cassette with earphones. My master taught me a healing method and mantra, while warning me not to use it for terminal cases. He said, "At one time when I used it in a terminal case, it took me seven years to overcome my resultant illness."

Also, do not grant such boons to those who will not devote their lives to a spiritual pursuit. I have found in my experiments that if one keeps repeating the same practice, it often becomes self-defeating and nothing gets accomplished. It is like saying, "Mother give me food," and she says, "I am serving it now." You may keep on saying, "Mother give me food," but she will give it only when she wishes to. Your pleadings are of no use.

How do I know how much *japa* is needed for a given purpose? It is written in the works on mantra-*shastra* but, again, in my experience, it is all a matter of learning by experimentation and refining the 'skill'. One may ask the guru within, but it is tricky to discern whether it is the guru who answers or if it is one's own silly and confused subconscious.

When you recite a mantra with an ulterior motive, for instance, the *mahalakshmi* mantra, let the *sankalpa* be:

Guru-pritya mahalakshmi-prity-artham

(Through the guru's pleasure, for the pleasure of Mahalakshmi)

That should suffice. Do not set other conditions, like, "Give me a million-dollar cheque." But do set this condition for yourself, "If Lady Luck is pleased with me, I shall give away at least 10 per cent of her gift. And thus, being freed of some part of the burden, I shall be able to fulfil my totally unselfish desire to serve others, for which I shall give 10 per cent of my time and energy to serve God, guru, deities and fellow beings." Otherwise you are asking the deities to serve you without giving them anything in return and they do not like this. Hence you will have to pay a price. So, look into the motive with great subtlety, purify and refine it as much as possible and serve the deity by reciting your *japa*.

Another question often asked is: What is the best time of the day to do *purash-charana*? Whatever time is convenient to you, preferably the morning is the best as the fixed time and is flexible for the rest.

There are certain days on which a practice may be started. A good astrologer will be able to guide you on that. For *yogis* the dates are not that important and I do not consult astrologers for the ones I do myself for the benefit of others. Also it is said: "*Mumukshunam sada kalah strinam kalash cha sarvada*" (For those seeking liberation [*moksha*] any time is permissible; for women also, any time is appropriate.) But, a certain level of purity is needed to benefit from such freedom.

The best path is to perform a *yajna*, a fire sacrifice. It is the most effective way of *japa*. But it is costly in terms of time and finance. A 1,25,000-*ahuti yajna* may cost up to $1,000 as cost of *ghee, samagree* (mixture of aromatic, curative, de-pollutant herbs and parts of plants and trees, available readymade) and fire, if done by oneself. If done through a priest, add the priest's offerings generously.

The priests, keepers of the tradition, will advise you on the performance of all sorts of *pujas*.

One needs to identify a special seat for the performance of *purash-charana*, and resolve to sit there at least once a day during the period of observance. For the purpose of intense practice, set aside a room that is darkened as much as possible, leaving perhaps the light of a candle. The curtains should be dark coloured, and if one is prone to get disturbed at external noise, one may soundproof the site as far as possible.

However, if one wants something accomplished for a specific home, or for an *ashram*, or an institution, then it is advantageous to perform the observance at that particular location. For example, if there is strife among the members of an institution, a qualified preceptor may choose to perform the *anu-shthana* at that location as it will create a peaceful collective mind-field. The same effect can be obtained hundredfold if 100 members undertake the practice at the same time.

On the other hand, one may withdraw to a guru's *ashram* to complete such an *anu-shthana* (observance). This has the added advantage that in case of any problems, one has the ready guidance from one's preceptor. The preceptor's presence is often conducive to discipline.

There are also special sacred places where one may perform the *purash-charanas* of particular mantras — the *mani-karnika ghat*, cremation ground, in Varanasi for *mrityujnjaya* mantra; the temple of Anasuya near Gopeshwar in the Garhwal Himalayas to seek a desired offspring; the Kanyakumari temple at the peninsular tip of India for doing a special version of *mrityunjaya* to obtain a desired husband; to Naina Devi temple to pray for curing an eye disease, or one may recite *Vishnu-sahasra-nama* (the thousand names of Vishnu) at Badrinath for the same purpose. To practice the special mantra of the guru-*chakra*, one can go to Tarakeshwar in the Garhwal Himalayas; and so on and so forth.

Here, a point arises that I have not often emphasised, or stated, for fear that it would be misinterpreted. No *yajna*, or sacramental act, is complete without a *dakshina*, a gift offering. It is a normal tradition in India, as also in other spiritual traditions, to make an offering to the priest and the preceptor. Ideally one can put aside 10 per cent, or even one per cent of one's income for the duration of the *purash-charana*. We often give such offerings coupled with clothes, fruit, or whatever else. It is not a business deal just as the *japa* is not. If one prefers, one may even make a donation to one's favourite charitable institution. Let it not be done with a feeling of burden but as an expression of love. This is also one of the secrets for becoming prosperous; give away one per cent, better still, 10 per cent, of all your energies as an unselfish anonymous donation. The rider is: Do not expect a return; it will return to you tenfold. However, in the case of priests specially employed, an extra offering to them or to the preceptor is optional. The blessings come from within oneself.

There are very strong traditions of coupling the mantra with other ascetic observances, such as silence, fasting, refraining from certain food items, a period of celibacy and so forth in varying degrees. Some non-vegetarians may become vegetarian during the period, or may refrain from *rajasic* and *tamasic* food like onions and garlic. Or they may refrain from eating salt and may eat only boiled food without spices. In fact, people in India and in some other countries like Thailand, invariably ask about what other disciplines they need to follow for the duration of the observance. Teaching in the West, we do not emphasise these disciplines of *sadhana* but deep inside, every preceptor longs to find students and disciples who would prefer to undertake such disciplines.

Even if one does not intentionally undertake such associative disciplines, quite often one finds a natural change in inclination during the mantra-observance. One may simply want to sleep, eat, speak, indulge less in sexual relations, without any prompting. Then these changed inclinations become pleasant experiences and cease to be enforced disciplines. As a result, this enhances the intensity of the mantra-observance and increases its fruit.

The word *purash-charana* means 'a step forward'. When one undertakes such observances, one takes a quantum leap on one's spiritual journey.

Swamiji, our Baba or Swami Rama of the Himalayas, used to say, "Six months before anything happens in the exterior world, some changes occur in the subtle world."

I have often found that the results of a special *purash-charana* may take up to six months to filter into the exterior world. So, do not finish the *japa* today and expect a jump in the Dow-Jones tonight. Surrender, carry on as though you had done nothing. That is important.

Lay claim to nothing.
Abandon thyself.

five

REFINING YOUR MANTRA

What is the meaning of the word 'cat'? What is the meaning of the word 'dog'? Is the word a translation into another language? Is that the meaning? Instead of saying 'man', if I said in French, '*l'homme*', then do I know the meaning? One word is not the same as another. The word signifies something, points to something. The Sanskrit word for an object, any object, any entity, any state, any object, is *padartha.* The word *padartha* itself means, "the meaning of the word". An object, whether concrete or abstract, is the meaning of the word. So what's the meaning of the word 'rug'? The meaning of the word is a silent pointing of the finger to the rug, and whatever you find there, through experience, that is the meaning of the word 'rug'. Whatever experience, concrete or abstract, a word points to, the word signifies that experience. And again, the meaning is concrete or abstract. So, whatever experience your mantra leads to, that *experience* is the meaning of your mantra. One redefinition we need to get used to is that there exist multi-level meanings of words, just as we have multi-level experiences of objects, whether concrete or abstract.

What do I mean by the multi-level experience of an object?

Take for example, the microphone I am wearing around my neck. To a person well versed in geometry or a student of shape and form or to an artist, it is a cylindrical shape. To an electronics expert it is a magnetic disc with an apparatus inside which converts sound into an electric current before converting that electric current back into magnetic vibrations in the magnetic disc in the speaker, where it is heard as a sound again. To a metallurgist, this microphone is a combination of metals; to a physicist, it's a field of energy made concrete in the form of atoms, electrons and molecules. But to a public speaker, it's just a microphone.

So, you take an object to gain its multi-level functions and multi-level experiences. The way a tailor looks at a shirt is not the same way a prospective bridegroom looks at it when buying the shirt. He wants to wear it. Each has a different experience of the same object. Not only that, we have multi-level experiences of the same object; for instance, a woman buys a dress. To make some alterations in it, she rips the seams apart and cuts out a portion and sews it. Her experience of the dress, at that time, is entirely different from her experience of that very dress when she wears it to a party. There are two different experiences, but the dress is the same. This is enhanced when we move from the concrete to the abstract. It becomes more refined, more powerful, more energetic, more pervasive because there is one cosmic law by which the subtle definer is always more powerful than the grosser, coarser. So as the experience of the mantra becomes more refined in the mind, its effect on us becomes more pervasive and its finer meanings become more manifest. By the word 'meaning' again, we mean the 'experience'. Take for example, the simple mantra you have practiced for many months: '*so-ham*', which simply means: 'I am that.' 'That' is what? Or in the *Bible*: "I am that I am"; now what is 'that'? We are constantly running after 'that' — that something over there, way away; that something that happened in the past; that something that will happen in the future; that thing in the neighbour's yard; that thing on somebody's back; that *other*, far away. We call it, in India, the attraction of the distant drums.

You hear the drums, your ears perk up, you want to run after 'that'. Throughout our lives we run after 'that' — something distant, something not within me, something that I am not, something I do not have or think I do not have. The meditative experience is the experience of unity. In fact, the word '*so-ham*' occurs first in a very ancient passage, dated somewhere between 3,000 and 4,000 years ago. The passage says, "The splendour that shines in the sun — *that* I am. So I am that which I have sought. In all my pursuits, it was the pursuit of the fulfilment of the self. In my cravings was hidden the craving for the knowledge of the self. I am that which I have been searching for in the things distant, in times distant, in pursuit of distant objects. Things that I thought were away, were within me."

Many philosophical texts expound on this philosophy. I do not know whether it is true or not, whether a naturalist would corroborate this or not, but one of the analogies given is of the musk deer, the smell of whose musk so overpowers him in the mountains, the Himalayas, that he runs crazily, trying to find the source of the fragrance. He goes around searching, smelling every object: 'Where is this smell coming from?' I don't know whether it is true or not, but that is the analogy I was made to read in the ancient philosophic texts. This is one meaning of '*so- ham*': "I am that; I am the splendour of the sun, all things distant."

But now we repeat, "*So-ham so-ham...*" It becomes *ham-so*. Some schools of yoga, in fact, refer to it as the *ham-so* mantra. The word means a white-winged swan: a pure, free flying, swan-like self. Which swan is it? '*Ham-so*' is synonymous with the sun: I am a solar being, shining like the sun. Or it is merely the sound of the breath, and the wings of the swan are the nostrils? So, as you unravel the meaning of the symbol in your personal experience, the meaning of the word changes.

I can go on speaking of the word '*so-ham*', and not stop; so it is with your mantra. Each syllable represents a ray of light, a ray of the sun of consciousness that shines within you. And each ray brings forth in you a burst of appropriate energies, and, when concentrated upon, helps to draw the energies you have dissipated. At the moment, our energies are dissipated in an excessive flow of emotions; excessive flow of sexuality, which sometimes makes us helpless; excessive flow of rationality, whereby we fail to love as we become so rational; so excessive a flow of plain kinetic energy that keeps us moving our hands and feet without any constructiveness, because we cannot relax, because we cannot draw that energy inwards that will make us still. And we think the more we move the more energetic we are — in fact, the more we move the more exhausted we become. In the *Bhagavad Gita*, or in the words of St. Teresa of Avila, a turtle always draws its limbs inwards, so too in prayer does the soul draw all its senses inwards, and the mantra becomes the centre of that in-drawing of energies, in making a still and yet powerful field of your energy's being, your life principle, your consciousness. It is not a *forced* stillness. It is not a tying down of yourself. It is simply a heightening of the field of your energies which you can then channelise by the use of a free will; not by the use of simple urges, reflexes, compulsions that leave you helpless.

Now, how do you refine your mantra so that it becomes an instrument of inspiration? Initially, you simply begin with an ordinary *japa*, or *japam*, which is simply the repetition of a mantra. But gradually we have to change the word into a mental vibration so that the word is hardly seen as a word any more. It takes a while to get there. Of course, as with any relationship, whatever you put of yourself into it, you are able to draw from it.

People ask sometimes: "How long do I have to keep meditating?"

So I reply "How long do you have to keep going to sleep every night? How long do you have to keep eating every day? How long do you have to keep brushing your teeth and showering your body?" It is a constant, regular, something new that you are adding to yourself, like brushing your teeth, like taking a shower. As your practice improves, it will benefit you. If you really try to attend group meditations at least once a week, you will not realise their benefits while attending to them. But when you miss one, you will realise its benefits. Your own concentration in the field of meditation should not be to seek the more advanced techniques to use; but within the technique, concentrate on *how well* you advance. Curiosity is natural to a human being, but discipline means keeping to one's practice and doing it over and over again.

As to the refining of the mantra, I'll give you two or three different ways in which you can refine the experience of the mantra. Take, for example, a syllable, a sound, the first letter of the Sanskrit, Arabic, Hebrew, Greek, Latin, English alphabet, the sound of the letter 'alpha', the sound: '*a*'. Now, just say the sound '*a*'. You have now said the sound '*a*' by force of habit without self-observation. It's almost a reflex, but to say '*a*', somewhere deep in the hidden recesses, the free will operates. Free will makes a choice for you every micro moment of the day — to say something, to cease saying it, to make a move, to cease the movement. This will is conscious. It is the core of your life and activity. It is the core of your consciousness.

This free will says, "All right, I decide. I have a choice: to say it or not to say it. Now, at this moment, I'll choose to say '*a*'."

So the free will says to the mind, "Okay, Mind, you will set the chain of vibrations going."

So your power of discrimination decides what chain of vibrations to receive from the mind. There is a tiny flicker of vibration in the mind; a vibration which is not yet a sound. It is the source of the sound; it is the vibration of an energy field — a very fine vibration of the mind that occurs in the mind and moves the physical energy in a corresponding area of the brain. A tiny electric storm in one part of the brain, a tiny release of sparks in the electricity of the brain occurs. Some sparks are wasted because we have not yet learned how to use the brain. While most of the electricity is wasted or lost, some is sent to the nerve channels. One message goes to a certain area of the abdomen where air is stored and the nerves say to the muscles: "Would you mind moving just a little, and release a little burst of air upwards?" So a little burst of air seeps upwards while at the same time, the message reaches the muscles of the throat.

The voice-box says, "I've sent a message down there to release a little burst of air. That air is coming up now; intercept it, watch it coming. Press the throat, contract it so much, open it so much and keep the tongue in position in relation to the teeth, the mouth, the lips, so that the position will produce the sound of '*a*'."

In anticipation of that burst coming, the throat, the voice-box, the tongue, the lips, the teeth, the jaw — everything is kept ready. At the burst of air, the tongue moves in the right proportion, the right way and there emerges the sound '*a*'. By the same process the tongue goes back to its original position. In this process of saying '*a*', several thousand neurological events take place. Just imagine the time factor involved in each of the billion neurological events taking place in the process of saying '*a*'!

Beyond the neurological events, what happens beyond the plane in the faculty of discrimination, in the free will, in your consciousness?

Here I would like you to say '*a*' again, watching it from the beginning of the act of your will till the production of the sound. The sounds are much softer than the previous time. Say it again. Watch the act of will all the way down.

Now, keeping the mouth sealed, just say '*a*' in your mind. Do not send the sound beyond the brain. You will sees that at the level of the brain, though the time span covered by that '*a*' is much shorter, the vibration is much finer.

A yoga master immersed in deep meditation is capable of experiencing something like a 600th part — 600 times as fine an experience — of the thought '*a*'. How fine is his neurological control? How fine is his perception of time, of space, of the sequences and causations and other principles that run the objects, alterations in the objects, experiences of the objects, experiences of life? When you practice your mantra, refine it and enter deeper into the source of your being. Observe how the will sends forth the thought. Observe it arising. Observe the process of each mantra being repeated in the mind.

You will need to spend some time on practicing the mantra with the breath. Making the breath as long and as fine as possible, exhale and inhale. By that refining of the breath, and with the mantra flowing out with each exhalation and flowing in with each inhalation, you will find it easier to reach the core of your mind. Now shift to the mental repetition of the *japa*. Let the mantra appear in the mind and become a remembrance. People say, "Well, it comes into my mouth, but is very difficult to be remembered mentally."

I don't see the reason for any difficulty. All the time you are engaged in silent thinking. If you let the thoughts reach your mouth, people would consider you crazy. If you can engage yourself in other thoughts, you can do the same with the mantra. For example, imagine that you are walking alone and suddenly you remember the name of a friend. You don't call the name out. The people around would wonder what's wrong with you! So, more than a repetition, the mantra should become a rememberance — something to remember in the back of your mind. Rememberance is not only when meditating, but all through the day. Refine the remembrance. Watch it. Watch how the thought arises and by what process. Each time you repeat the memory of the mantra, observe: observe the mind, observe the mantra. Do it with a relaxed body, without tension. When you have done the refining of the mantra for some time, with or without the *mala* beads, come back to the breath and the mantra at the same time.

A great many people pay attention to the mantra and to its each syllable. This is fine initially, but gradually your mantra should become a part of the superconscious mind. It is one complete unit and the syllables are parts of a seed. In the seed, where are the branches, the twigs, the leaves of the tree? They are all there as one single unit. That is why the word 'bead' in a string of *mala* is derived from the Sanskrit word meaning 'seed' and the most important mantras are known as seed syllables. The mantra should move in your mind as a bead turning over and over. As the bead of the *mala* turns, it only follows the *beeja*, the mantra in the field of your mind. The entire mantra then becomes one single unit responsible for a spontaneous vibration.

appendix

If, for example, the author's close friend, the late Dr Usharbudh Arya had performed a Vedic ceremony of undertaking an observance (*anu-shthana*) in Rishikesh on 25 December 1993 at noon, he would have recited a *sankalpa* with is paraphrased thus:

Here,

all creation being in his imagination and knowledge,
who is the substratum of all —

the very self comprising the essence of existence,
consciousness and bliss

playing forth with his supreme *shakti*, his original Lady
Nature,

endowed with unthinkable, immeasurable, infinite
potencies and powers,

the great Lord, Narayana, the Spirit meditation upon
the waters,

He of infinite power,

among His many trillions of universes spinning in the vast ocean of forces,

in this sector of the universe, veiled in unmanifest matter and its manifestations:

cosmic intelligence, cosmic ego, earth, water, light, air, space, and many more;

upholds a thousand galaxies: the hoods of *Shesha*, King of Serpents.

Among those thousand snake-hood galaxies, on one of those hoods

is a tiny mustard seed: the earth, situated between the seven worlds above and the seven layers that are the worlds below.

Supported by eight guardian forces in each of the eight directions,

held firm by the axis-mountain Sumeru and others,

constituted of seven great continents which are surrounded by seven seas all joined by the latitudes and longitudes.

On this particular continent (*Jambu-dvipa* by name) are nine sub-continents;

among them, Bharata, unique and most favoured by the gods,

comprising 46 provinces, numerous forests with nine major ones and 24 major rivers, above the equator, to the west of the holy land of

Kurukshetra, between the Rivers Yamuna and Ganga,
in the precincts of such *ashrams* as Badrinath,
at the *ashram* of Swami Rama in the holy city of Rishikesh.

Now,

calculated according to the systems established by sages such as Garga and Varaha, in Brahma's day in the forenoon,
in the cycle of creation known as the *kalpa* of the White Boar,
in the seventh of 14 *manu* intervals, known as *vaivasvata*, in the first quarter of the 28th *kali yuga*, during the Buddha incarnation, in the year called, 1955885093 years of the current creation era having elapsed, 5093 of the *Kali* era having elapsed,
2049 years of the era of Emperor Vikramaditya having elapsed (and you may choose to add any other national or local era)
in the year named *Parthiva* (1993-94) during the northern passage of the sun above the equator,
in the month of the eighth lunar mansion on the fourth day of the month of the constellation.
Pushya (Aldabaran) in the solar calendar, on the twelfth day of the bright fortnight of the month whose constellation is *Mrgashiras*, on Saturday,

in the *Krittikas* (Pleiades) constellation in the Scorpio sign of the Zodiac (and some finer calculations of *yoga* and *karana* are being omitted here),

the sun being in Sagittarius, the moon in Aries, Mercury in Sagittarius, Guru (Jupiter) in Libra, Venus in Sagittarius, Saturn in Aquarius, Rahu in Scorpio, and Ketu in Taurus,

at the seventh of 30 divisions of day and night, the *muhurta* named *Vishva-deva*.

I,

born in the lineage of Sage Bharadvaja,

in the tradition of *Yajur-Veda*, of the Vajasaneya recension,

great-grandson of NN, grandson of NN, son of NN, to confer sacred *karma* to 10 past and 10 future and thus 21 generations,

holding the deities, sacred fires, priests and gurus as my witnesses,

for the pleasure of my guru-lineage and to please my *ishta-devata*,

for the fulfilment of *dharma*, *artha*, *kama* and *moksha*,

I make this resolve, I undertake this sacred observance.

May it be my surrendered offering to Brahman.

some mantras to chant

MORNING MANTRA

GURU MANTRA

Verses 1 and 2 are from the *Guru Gītā* in the *Skanda-Purāṇa* and Verse 3 is composed by Swāmi Veda Bhāratī for the frontispiece to his *Yoga Sūtras* (Volume I: *Samādhi-pāda*)

Verse 1

ॐ ॐ ॐ गुरुर्ब्रह्मा गुरुर्विष्णुर्गुरुर्देवो महेश्वरः ।
गुरुः साक्षात्परं ब्रह्म तस्मै श्रीगुरवे नमः ॥

Om Om Om guru brahmā gurur viṣṇur gurur devo
maheśvaraḥ, guruḥ sākṣāt paraṁ brahma
tasmai śrī-gurave namaḥ.

Om, Om, Om, to that beautiful and benevolent guru who is Brahmā, the creator, Viṣṇu, the maintainer, and Śiva, the Great Lord through whom all things return to their origin. To that guru who is the direct experience of Brahman; salutations.

Verse 2

अखण्डमण्डलाकारं व्याप्तं येन चराचरम्।
तत्पदं दर्शितं येन तस्मै श्रीगुरवे नमः ॥

Akhaṇḍa-maṇḍalākāraṁ vyāptaṁ yena carācaram,
tat-padaṁ darśitaṁ yena tasmai śrī-gurave namaḥ.

(Which) pervades the entire unbroken form of the circle (of creation), moving and unmoving. To that beautiful and benevolent guru through whom that state was revealed (to me); salutations.

Verse 3

हिरण्यगर्भादारब्धां शेषव्यासादिमध्यमाम्।
स्वामिश्रीराम पादान्तां वन्दे गुरु परम्पराम् ॥

Hiraṇya-garbhād ārabdhāṃ śeṣa-vyāsādi-madhyamām,
svāmi-śri-rāmā-pādāntāṁ vande guru-paramparām.

Originating from the golden womb (of light, the guru-spirit), and (flowing) down through the medium of gurus like Śeṣa (Patañjali), Vyāsa and the rest, ending at the feet of Srī Svāmi Rāma, that (unbroken stream of) succession, I worship.

PEACE MANTRA

This Śānti-Pāṭha is a traditional introduction to several of the *Upaniṣads*.

ॐ असतो मा सद्गमय। तमसो मा ज्योतिर्गमय।
मृत्योर्मा अमृतं गमय ॥

Om asato mā sad gamaya,
tamaso mā jyotir gamaya,
mṛtyor mā amṛtaṁ gamaya.

ॐ शान्तिः शान्तिः शान्तिः ॥
Om śantiḥ śāntiḥ śāntiḥ.

Om, lead me from the unreal and the untrue to the real and true. Lead me from darkness (of ignorance) unto light (of consciousness). Lead me from mortality to immortality. *Om*, peace, peace, peace.

MANTRA AT DAWN BY ŚANKARĀCĀRYA

(Prātaḥ-smaraṇa-stotram)

Verse 1

प्रातः स्मरामि हृदि संस्फुरदात्मतत्त्वं सच्चित्सुखं परमहंसगतिं तुरीयम् ।
यत् स्वप्नजागरसुषुप्तिमवैति नित्यं तद्ब्रह्म निष्कलमहं न च भूतसङ्घः॥

Prātaḥ smarāmi hṛdi saṃsphurad-ātma-tattvaṃ
sac-cit-sukhaṁ parama-haṃsa-gatiṁ turīyam,
yat svapna-jāgara-suṣuptim avaiti nityaṁ
tad brahma niṣkalaṁ ahaṁ na ca bhūta-saṅghaḥ.

At dawn I remember the true self, shining in the heart, the fourth state, *turīya*, existence-consciousness-supreme joy, the goal of the supreme sages, that which eternally pervades the three (other states) — waking, dream and deep sleep. I am that eternal Brahman; not this aggregate of elements.

Verse 2

प्रातर्भजामि मनसां वचसामगम्यं वाचो विभान्ति निखिला यदनुग्रहेण।
यन्नेति नेति वचनैर्निगमा अवोचंस् तं देवदेवमजमच्युतमाहुरग्र्यम् ॥

Prātar bhajāmi manasāṁ vacasām agamyaṁ
vāco vibhānti nikhilā yad-anugraheṇa,
yan neti neti vacanair nigamā avocaṃs
taṁ deva-devam ajam acyutam āhur agryam.

At dawn I sing the praise of that which is unreachable for the mind and words; that by whose grace all words shine; that which the scriptures describe with the words, "neither this nor that", that unborn, eternal, foremost Divinity of divinities.

Verse 3

प्रातर्नमामि तमसः परमर्कवर्णं पूर्णं सनातनपदं पुरुषोत्तमाख्यम्।
यस्मिन्निदं जगदशेषमशेषमूर्तौ रज्ज्वां भुजङ्गम इव प्रतिभासितं वै ॥

Prātar namāmi tamasaḥ param arka-varṇaṁ
pūrṇaṃ sanātana-padaṁ puruṣottamākhyam,
yasminn idaṁ jagad aśeṣam aśeṣa-mūrtau
rajjvāṁ bhujaṅgama iva prati-bhāsitaṁ vai.

At dawn, I bow to that whose colour is a flash beyond darkness (of the void, *śunya*, or of ignorance), the plenum, the ancient goal (of eternal state), which is called the ultimate person (hoof); that in which the remainder (whole of the) Universe is revealed as the rope, instead of the serpent.

Verse 4

श्लोकत्रयमिदं पुण्यं लोकत्रयविभूषणम् ।
प्रातःकाले पठेद्यस्तु स गच्छेत् परमं पदम् ॥

Śloka-trayam idaṁ puṇyaṁ loka-tarya-vibhūṣaṇam,
prātaḥ-kāle paṭhed yas tu sa gacchet paramaṁ padam.

Whosoever at the dawning hour recites this auspicious triad of verses, an ornament to the three worlds, goes to the supreme station — *mokṣa*, liberation.

MANTRA FOR HARMONY BETWEEN TEACHER AND STUDENT

This *Śanti-Pāṭha* is a traditional introduction to several of the *Upaniṣads.*

ॐ सह नाववतु । सह नौ भुनक्तु । सह वीर्यं करवावहै ।
तेजस्वि नावधीतमस्तु । मा विद्विषावहै ॥

Om saha nāv avatu, saha nau bhunaktu,
saha vīryaṁ karavāvahai, tejasvi nāv adhītam astu,
mā vidviṣāvahai.

ॐ शान्तिः शान्तिः शान्तिः ॥
Om śāntiḥ śāntiḥ śāntiḥ.

Om, may It (Brahman) protect us both together. May It (Brahman) enjoy/feed us both together. May we create spiritual power together. May what we have studied together be possessed of brilliance. May we not hate one another. *Om,* peace, peace, peace.

MANTRA OF COMPLETION

This *Śanti-Pāṭha* is a traditional introduction to the *Iṣā Upaniṣad.*

ॐ पूर्णमदः पूर्णमिदं पूर्णात्पूर्णमुदच्यते ।
पूर्णस्य पूर्णमादाय पूर्णमेवावशिष्यते ॥

Om pūrṇam adaḥ pūrṇam idaṁ pūrṇāt pūrṇam
udacyate, pūrṇasya pūrṇam ādāya
pūrṇam evāva-śiṣyate.

ॐ शान्तिः शान्तिः शान्तिः ॥
Om śāntiḥ śāntiḥ śāntiḥ.

Om, that is full/complete/perfect. This is full/complete/perfect. Perfection arises from the perfect. Taking the perfect of the perfect, it remains as the perfect alone. *Om,* peace, peace, peace.

EVENING MANTRA
Śiva-Saṅkalpa-Sūktam

(*Yajur Veda*)

ॐ यज्जाग्रतो दूरमुदैति दैवं तदु सुप्तस्य तथैवैति।
दूरङ्गमं ज्योतिषां ज्योतिरेकं तन्मे मनः शिवसङ्कल्पमस्तु ॥

Om yaj jāgrato dūram udaiti daivaṁ
tadu suptasya tathaivaiti,
dūraṅgamaṁ jyotiṣāṁ jyotir ekaṁ
tan me manaḥ śiva-saṅkalpam astu. (I)

Om, that may mind of mine be auspicious resolution, which goes farther off (than other sense organs, like eye, etc.); when one is awakening which alone is the perceiver of the soul; which comes back in the same way in which it goes away when it is sleeping; which is far going and which is the soul of all external organs.

येन कर्माण्यपसो मनीषिणो यज्ञे कृण्वन्ति विदथेषु धीराः।
यदपूर्वं यक्षमन्तः प्रजानां तन्मे मनः शिवसङ्कल्पमस्तु ॥

Yena karmāṇy-apaso manīṣiṇo
yajñe kṛṇvanti vidatheṣu dhīrāḥ
yad apūrvaṁ yakṣam antaḥ prajānāṁ
tan me manaḥ śiva-saṅkalpam astu. (II)

That may mind of mine be auspicious resolution, through which resolute and intelligent men, devoted to the performance of religious rights, do their work in sacrifice and worship, which is unprecedented, (which is) capable of performing sacrifice and (which is) present in the body of all living beings.

यत्प्रज्ञानमुत चेतो धृतिश्च यज्जयोतिरन्तरमृतं प्रजासु ।
यस्मान्न ऋते किञ्चन कर्म क्रियते तन्मे मनः शिवसङ्कल्पमस्तु ॥

Yat prajñānam uta ceto dhṛtiś ca
yaj jyotir antar amṛaṁ prajāsu,
yasmān na ṛte kiñcana karma kriyate
tan me manaḥ śiva-saṅkalpam astu. (III)

That may mind of mine be auspicious resolution, which is the instrument of gaining special and general knowledge, which is steadiness itself, which is the immortal light in living being (that directs the external organs to their respective objects) and without which no work is possible.

येनेदं भूतं भुवनं भविष्यत् परिगृहीतममृतेन सर्वम् ।
येन यज्ञस्तायते सप्त होता तन्मे मनः शिवसङ्कल्पमस्तु ॥

Yenedaṁ bhūtaṁ bhuvanaṁ bhaviṣyat
pari-gṛhītam amṛtena sarvam,
yena yajñas tāyate sapta hotā
tan me manaḥ śiva-śaṅkalpam astu. (IV)

That may mind of mine be auspicious resolution,

which is immortal, by which everything is known in this world in present, past, and future, and by which the sacrifice presided over by seven priests, is performed.

यस्मिन्नृचः साम यजूँषि यस्मिन् प्रतिष्ठिता रथनाभाविवाराः।
यस्मिंश्चित्तगुँ सर्वमोतं प्रजानां तन्मे मनः शिवसङ्कल्पमस्तु ॥

Yasminn ṛcaḥ sāma yajūguṁṣi yasmin
pratiṣṭhitā ratha-nābhāvivārāh,
yasmiṃś cittaguṁ sarvam otaṁ prajānāṁ
tan me manaḥ śiva-saṅkalpam astu. (V)

That may mind of mine be auspicious resolution, in which the *Ṛg-Veda*, the *Sāma-Veda*, and the *Yajur-Veda* are set up like the nave of a wheel and, in which, all knowledge of living beings is woven.

सुषारथिरेश्वानिव यन्मनुष्यान् नेनीयतेऽभीशुभिर्वाजिन इव।
हृत्प्रतिष्ठं यदजिरं जविष्ठं तन्मे मनः शिवसङ्कल्पमस्तु ॥

Suṣārathir aśvān iva yan manuṣyān
nenīyate bhīśubhir vājina iva,
hṛt-pratiṣṭhaṁ yad ajiraṁ javiṣṭhaṁ
tan me manaḥ śiva-śaṅkalpam astu. (VI)

ॐ शान्तिः शान्तिः शान्तिः ॥
Om śāntiḥ śāntiḥ śāntiḥ.

That may mind of mine be auspicious resolution, which impels living beings here and there, and controls them as a good charioteer does to horses; which resides in heart and is never old and which is very swift. *Om*, peace, peace, peace.

GURU MANTRA

This verse is from the *Guru Gitā* in the *Skanda-Purāṇa.*

ॐ ॐ ॐ गुरुर्ब्रह्मा गुरुर्विष्णुर्गुरुर्देवो महेश्वरः।
गुरुः साक्षात्परं ब्रह्म तस्मै श्रीगुरवे नमः ॥

Om Om Om guru brahmā gurur viṣṇur gurur devo
maheśvaraḥ, guruḥ sākṣāt paraṁ brahma
tasmai śrī-gurave namaḥ.

To that beautiful and benevolent guru who is Brahma, the creator, Viṣṇu, the maintainer, and Śiva, the great Lord through whom all things return to their origin. To that guru who is the direct experience of Brahman; salutations.

PEACE MANTRA

This *Śānti-Pāṭha* is a traditional introduction to several of the *Upaniṣads.*

असतो मा सद्गमय।
तमसो मा ज्योतिर्गमय। मृत्योर्मा अमृतं गमय ॥

Asato mā sad gamaya, tamaso mā jyotir gamaya,
mṛtyor mā amṛtaṁ gamaya.

Lead me from the unreal and the untrue to the real and true. Lead me from darkness (of ignorance) unto light (of consciousness). Lead me from mortality to immortality.

VERSES FROM ŚANKARĀCĀRYA

Saundarya Lahari (1, 3, 8)

Verse 1

शिवः शक्त्या युक्तो यदि भवति शक्तः प्रभवितुं
न चेदेवं देवो न खलु कुशलः स्पन्दितुमपि।
अतस्त्वामाराध्यां हरिहरविरिञ्चयादिभिरपि
प्रणन्तुं स्तोतुं वा कथमकृतपुण्यः प्रभवति॥

Śivaḥ śaktyā yukto yadi bhavati śaktaḥ pra-bhavituṁ
na ced evaṁ devo na khalu kuśalaḥ spanditum api,
ataṣ tvām ārādhyāṁ hari-hara-viriñcy-ādibhir api
pranaṇtuṁ stotuṁ vā katham akṛta-punyaḥ
prabhavati.

If Śiva is united with Śakti, he is able to exert his powers as Lord. If not, the God is not able to stir. How can one who has not acquired merit be fit to offer reverence and praise to you, who must be propitiated by Hari, Hara, Viriñci and the others (gods, the Divine powers of creation, maintenance and dissolution)?

Verse 3

अविद्यानामन्तस्तिमिरमिहिरद्वीपनगरी
जडानां चैतन्यस्तबकमकरन्दश्रुतिसृतिः।
दरिद्राणां चिन्तामणिगुणनिका जन्मजलधौ
निमग्नानां दंष्ट्रा मुररिपुवराहस्य भवती॥

Avidyānām antas timira-mihira-dvīpa-nagarī
jaḍānāṁ caitanya-stabaka-makaranda-śruti-sṛtiḥ

daridrāṇāṁ cintā-maṇi-guṇanikā janma-jaladhau
nimagnānāṁ daṃṣṭrā mura-ripu-varāhasya bhavatī.

You are the island-city of the sun, (dispelling) the darkness of the ignorant. For the mentally stagnant, you are a waterfall of streams of nectar (flowing) from streams of consciousness. For the poor, you are the (duplicate of Indra's) wishing jewel. For those submerged in the ocean of birth (and death), you are the tusk of that boar (Viṣṇu as the boar incarnation) who was the enemy of Mura.

Verse 8

सुधासिन्धोर्मध्ये सुरविटपिवाटीपरिवृते
मणिद्वीपे नीपोपवनवति चिन्तामणिगृहे ।
शिवाकारे मञ्चे परमशिवपर्यङ्कनिलयां
भजन्ति त्वां धन्याः कतिचन चिदानन्दलहरीम् ॥

Sudhā-sindhor madhye sura-viṭapi-vāṭi-parivṛte
maṇi-dvīpe nipopavanavati cintā-maṇi-gṛhe,
śivākāre mañce parama-śiva-paryaṅka-nilayāṁ
bhajanti tvāṁ dhanyāḥ katicana cid ānanda-laharīm.

ॐ शान्तिः शान्तिः शान्तिः ॥
Om śāntiḥ śāntiḥ śāntiḥ.

Some few lucky ones worship you, a flood of consciousness and supreme bliss, your seat a mattress which is Parama Śiva, on a couch composed of the four gods, Śiva (and the others), in the mansion of wishing jewels with its grove of *Nīpa* trees, in the Isle of Gems, covered with groves of heavenly wish-fulfilling trees, in the midst of the ocean of nectar. *Om*, peace, peace, peace.

MEAL MANTRA

The third verse of this prayer is Verse 24 of the fourth chapter of the *Bhagavad Gītā*. The last line of the prayer may also be used at the end of practice to dedicate the fruits of one's meditation to the welfare of all.

ॐ अन्नपूर्णे सदापूर्णे शङ्करप्राणवल्लभे ।
ज्ञानवैराग्यसिद्ध्यर्थं भिक्षां देहि च पार्वति ॥

Om anna-pūrṇe sadāpūrṇe śaṅkara-prāṇa vallabhe,
jñāna-vairāgya-siddhyarthaṁ bhikṣāṁ dehi ca pārvati.

O Parvati, source of all that is nourishing, source of never-ending abundance, and Śankara's beloved consort, bestow upon us your blessing that will lead us into perfect knowledge and wisdom.

माता तु पार्वती देवी पिता देवो महेश्वरः ।
बान्धवाः शिवभक्ताश्च स्वदेशो भुवनत्रयम् ॥

Mātā tu Pārvatī devī pitā devo maheśvaraḥ,
bāndhavāḥ Śiva-bhaktāś ca sva-deśo bhuvana-trayam.

O Parvati, you are our Divine Mother, as Śiva is our Divine Father, and as fellow-worshippers of Śiva, inhabiting the three worlds, you are our brothers.

ब्रह्मार्पणं ब्रह्म हविर्ब्रह्माग्नौ ब्रह्मणा हुतम् ।
ब्रह्मैव तेन गन्तव्यं ब्रह्मकर्मसमाधिना ॥

Brahmārpaṇaṁ brahmahavir brahmāgnau brahmaṇā
hutam, brahmaiva tena gantavyaṁ
brahma-karma samādhinā.

Brahman the offering, Brahman the oblation; by Brahman poured into the fire of Brahman, Brahman is attained by one whose meditation is focused on action in Brahman.

ॐ विश्वात्मा प्रीयताम् ।
Om viśvātmā prīyatām,
ॐ तत्सद् ब्रह्मार्पणमस्तु ।
Om tat sad brahmārpaṇam astu,
ॐ शान्तिः शान्तिः शान्तिः ॥
Om śāntiḥ śāntiḥ śāntiḥ.

Om, may the universal self be satisfied. *Om*, that (Brahman) is truth, existence. May this be an offering to (that) Brahman. *Om*, peace, peace, peace.